Pasta Sensations

Tupperware invites you to bring on the pasta. This exciting collection of recipes—including savory sauces, robust main dishes, and easy-to-fix pasta side dishes—offers delicious possibilities for every occasion. And, many of the recipes can be prepared in 30 minutes or less, so you get great taste without spending a great deal of time. Start with Summer Vegetables with Linguine, shown on the cover, then cook your way through the recipes in the book. You'll delight in every fabulous forkful.

Produced by Meredith Publishing Services, 1912 Grand Avenue, Des Moines, IA 50309-3379.

This seal assures you that every recipe in **Pasta Sensations** has been tested in the *Better Homes and Gardens*® Test Kitchen. This means that each recipe is practical and reliable, and meets high standards of taste appeal.

All microwave recipes were tested in a variety of high-wattage microwave ovens. Cooking times are approximate since microwave ovens vary by manufacturer.

Tupperware™

Contents

Pasta
Potpourri

Simple, yet versatile, pasta is the perfect ingredient. Team it with meats, poultry, seafood, eggs, cheese, or vegetables. No matter how you prepare it, pasta will give you mouth-watering results. To help you get the most from pasta, here are some handy tips.

What Is Pasta?

A shaped dough made from flour, a liquid, and sometimes eggs, pasta can be made fresh at home or purchased dried, refrigerated, or frozen, and can be flavored with herbs, vegetables, or spices. The basic kinds of pasta are:

•*Egg Pasta:* Most homemade pastas and some commercial products are made from egg doughs. Many of the commercial versions that contain eggs are called noodles.

•*Macaroni Products:* These pastas usually are manufactured commercially because they require machines to form special shapes, such as elbows, shells, or wagon wheels. They typically are made using just flour and water.

•*Filled Pasta:* Most often made from egg doughs, these pastas have meat or cheese fillings. Tortellini and ravioli are two common filled pastas.

Pick a Pasta Shape

When choosing pasta, consider how ingredients and sauces will complement the pasta's shape. If you want to spoon on a sauce, use medium shells, corkscrew macaroni, long strands such as spaghetti, or medium tubes such as rigatoni. Layer wide, flat pastas such as lasagna noodles or stuff large hollow pastas such as manicotti and jumbo shells. For soups, rely on small pastas such as tiny bows or small shells. Serve filled pastas such as ravioli or tortellini with a simple sauce or bake them in a sauce with a covering of cheese. (See the tip on page 17 for hints on matching pastas and sauces.)

How Much Is Enough

When serving pasta with a sauce, remember these rules of thumb. For packaged dried pasta, use 2 ounces for a main-dish serving and 1 ounce for a side-dish serving. For homemade or refrigerated pasta, plan on 4 ounces for a main-dish serving and 2 ounces for a side-dish serving.

To measure uncooked packaged dried pasta, try these general guidelines. For small pastas, such as elbow macaroni or small shells, 1 cup weighs about 4 ounces. Medium pastas, such as cavatelli, rigatoni, or wagon wheels, weigh in at about 3 ounces to the cup. And for larger pastas, such as large bow ties and all noodles, 1 cup weighs about 2 ounces. To measure long pasta strands, such as vermicelli, linguine, or spaghetti, gather the pasta into a bunch. A 1-inch-diameter bunch will weigh about 4 ounces.

Storing Pasta

For best results, store packaged dried pasta in a cool, dry place in an airtight container, such as a Tupperware® Modular Mates® container. The pasta should last indefinitely. Store dried homemade or commercial refrigerated pasta in an airtight Tupperware refrigerator container in the refrigerator for up to three days. Or, freeze fresh homemade or commercial refrigerated pasta in a Tupperware Freezer Mates® container for up to eight months.

Serve It Right

For attractive, piping-hot pasta every time you serve it, use these pasta-handling tips.

Warm your serving dish by filling it with hot water and letting it stand a few minutes to absorb the heat. Once you've drained the pasta, quickly empty the dish and wipe it dry. Immediately place the pasta in the dish.

If you don't serve the pasta right away, cover it to keep it warm or return it to the hot cooking pan (but place the pan on a cool burner to avoid burning the pasta). For the best flavor, to avoid overcooking, and to keep the pasta from sticking, hold the pasta no longer than 10 minutes and stir it once or twice.

To serve up separate strands of long pastas, such as spaghetti or fettuccine, use two forks or the Tupperware Pasta Server to mound the pasta onto plates.

Pasta Identification

Supermarkets and specialty food stores offer a wide range of shapes, sizes, and flavors of pastas. To help you identify pasta shapes, take a look at this pictorial sampling. It includes the most common types of packaged dried, fresh, refrigerated, and frozen pasta shapes. You'll also notice a few flavored pastas, such as tomato and spinach fettuccine and tricolor corkscrew macaroni.

For several of the pastas, two names are listed because some manufacturers use Italian names while others use English names. As you shop for pasta, you may find pasta with names that differ from those listed here. When you do, make your selection based on shape and size rather than name.

Mafalda
(¾-inch-wide ribbons)

Fusilli
(twisted spaghetti)

Ziti
(long tubular pasta)

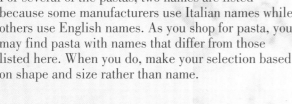

Small Shells
(conchigliette)

Medium/Large Shells
(conchiglie)

Tortellini
(little stuffed rings)

Tiny Bows
(tripolini)

Bow Ties or Butterflies
(farfalle)

Ravioli
(stuffed pasta squares)

Corkscrew Macaroni
(rotelle)

Rope Macaroni
(gemelli)

Lasagna Noodles
(2-inch-wide ribbons)

Fettuccine
(¼-inch-wide ribbons)

Jumbo Shells
(conchiglioni)

Rigatoni
(ridged pasta tubes)

Manicotti Shells
(large, diagonally cut tubes)

Linguine
(⅛-inch-wide ribbons)

Spaghetti
(round, thin strands)

Vermicelli
(thin spaghetti)

Mostaccioli or Penne
(smooth pasta tubes resembling quill pens)

Wagon Wheels
(ruote)

Cavatelli
(curled shells with ridges)

Spaghettini
(very thin spaghetti)

Orzo or Rosamarina
(ricelike pasta)

Acini di Pepe
(little peppercorns)

Rings
(anelli)

Angel Hair Pasta
(capellini)

7

Homemade Pasta

Per serving:
313 cal. (13% from fat), 11 g pro., 56 g carbo., 4 g fat,
107 mg cholesterol, 2 g dietary fiber, 300 mg sodium.

Preparation time:
30 minutes

Shaping time:
45 minutes

To make Homemade Pasta easier, use your food processor—it kneads the pasta dough for you. Place the steel blade in the food processor bowl. Add *all* of the flour, the salt, and the eggs. Cover and process until the mixture is the consistency of cornmeal. With the processor running, slowly pour the water and oil through the feed tube. Continue processing just until the dough forms a ball. Cover the dough and let rest 10 minutes. Shape and cook pasta as directed.

2   cups all-purpose flour

1   teaspon dried basil, marjoram, or sage, crushed (optional)

½   teaspoon salt

2   beaten eggs

⅓   cup water

1   teaspoon olive or cooking oil

⅓   cup all-purpose flour

- Mix the 2 cups flour, the herb (if using), and salt. Make a well in center of mixture. Mix eggs, water, and oil. Add to flour mixture; mix well. Sprinkle kneading surface with some of the ⅓ cup flour. Turn dough out onto floured surface. Knead dough until smooth and elastic (8 to 10 minutes total). Cover; let rest for 10 minutes. Divide dough into fourths.

- On floured surface, roll each fourth into a 12-inch square. Let stand for 20 minutes or until slightly dry. (Or, to use a pasta machine, pass each fourth of the dough through machine, according to manufacturer's directions, until ¹⁄₁₆ inch thick.) Shape as desired (see tip, below).

- If not using the pasta immediately, hang it from a pasta drying rack or clothes hanger, or spread it flat on a wire rack. Let dry overnight or until completely dry. Place the pasta in a Tupperware® refrigerator container; seal container and refrigerate up to 3 days. Or, to freeze the pasta, dry pasta at least 1 hour. Seal it in a Tupperware Freezer Mate® container and freeze for up to 8 months.

- Cook pasta according to directions on opposite page. Drain well. Makes 1 pound.

Three-Pepper Pasta: Cook ¾ cup chopped *red sweet pepper* in a small amount of *boiling water* for 10 to 15 minutes or until very tender. Drain well. In a blender container or food processor bowl, blend or process pepper until smooth; mixture should measure ⅓ cup. Stir 1½ teaspoons coarsely *ground black pepper* and ¼ teaspoon *ground red pepper* into pepper mixture. Prepare pasta as directed above, *except* use only *3 tablespoons* water and add pepper mixture to egg mixture. (The nutrition information per serving is the same as above *except:* 320 cal., 58 g carbo., 3 g dietary fiber.)

Shaping Pasta

Cut rolled dough for Homemade Pasta into one of these shapes:

Linguine or Fettuccine: Loosely roll up dough jelly-roll style; cut into ⅛-inch slices for linguine or ¼-inch slices for fettuccine. Shake strands to separate. Cut into even lengths.

Lasagna Noodles: Cut into strips 2 to 2½ inches wide. Then cut into desired lengths.

Bows: Cut into 2x1-inch rectangles or 1-inch circles. Pinch centers to form bows.

Cooking Pasta

In a large saucepan or Dutch oven, bring water (about 3 quarts of water for 4 to 8 ounces of pasta) to boiling. If desired, add 1 tablespoon olive or cooking oil (to help keep the pasta separated) and 1 teaspoon salt. Add pasta a little at a time so the water does not stop boiling. (Hold long pasta, such as spaghetti, at one end and dip other end into the water. As the pasta softens, curl it into the water.)

Reduce the heat slightly. Boil pasta, uncovered, for the time specified or until the pasta is al dente (tender but slightly firm). Stir occasionally. Test the pasta often for doneness near the end of the cooking time. Immediately drain the cooked pasta in a colander.

For recipes that specify rinsing, be sure to drain the pasta, rinse it under cold running water, and drain the pasta again. (Rinsing helps keep the pasta from overcooking and from sticking together.)

Note: To substitute homemade or refrigerated pasta for packaged dried pasta, use twice as much homemade or refrigerated pasta as dried pasta called for in a recipe.

Packaged Dried Pasta

Type of Pasta	Cooking Time
Acini di pepe	5 to 6 minutes
Angel hair pasta (capellini)	5 to 6 minutes
Bow ties or butterflies, medium (farfalle)	10 minutes
Bows, tiny (tripolini)	5 to 6 minutes
Cavatelli	12 minutes
Corkskrew macaroni (rotelle)	8 to 10 minutes
Elbow macaroni	10 minutes
Fettuccine	8 to 10 minutes
Fusilli	15 minutes
Lasagna noodles	10 to 12 minutes
Linguine	8 to 10 minutes
Mafalda	10 to 12 minutes
Manicotti shells	18 minutes
Mostaccioli or Penne	14 minutes
Noodles, fine, medium, or wide	6 to 8 minutes
Orzo or Rosamarina	5 to 8 minutes
Rigatoni	15 minutes
Rings (anelli)	9 to 10 minutes
Rope macaroni (gemelli)	10 minutes
Shells, jumbo (conchiglioni)	23 to 25 minutes
Shells, medium to large (conchiglie)	12 to 14 minutes
Shells, small (conchigliette)	8 to 9 minutes
Spaghetti	10 to 12 minutes
Spaghettini	8 to 10 minutes
Tortellini	15 minutes
Vermicelli	5 to 7 minutes
Wagon wheels (ruote)	12 minutes
Ziti	14 to 15 minutes

Homemade or Refrigerated Pasta

Use these times for homemade pasta—fresh, dried, or frozen—as well as for packaged refrigerated pasta.

Type of Pasta	Cooking Time
Bows	2 to 3 minutes
Fettuccine	1½ to 2 minutes
Lasagna noodles	2 to 3 minutes
Linguine	1½ to 2 minutes
Ravioli	6 to 8 minutes
Tortellini	8 to 10 minutes

Savory
Sauces

A rich sauce crowning a plate of steaming pasta—what could be more tempting? In this chapter, you'll find an array of sensational main-dish sauces, from robust chunky Marinara Sauce to smooth and subtly flavored Smoked Salmon Cream Sauce. Whether you serve these sauces for everyday meals or special occasions, they're quick to prepare—and are even quicker to disappear from everyone's plate.

Chicken and Red Pepper Sauce
over carrot fettuccine
(See recipe, page 12.)

Chicken and Red Pepper Sauce

Per serving:
503 cal. (31% from fat), 34 g pro., 53 g carbo., 17 g fat,
87 mg cholesterol, 3 g dietary fiber, 748 mg sodium.

**Preparation time:
30 minutes**

Serve this rich soup-based sauce over carrot fettuccine for a meal elegant enough for company. Round out your menu with a salad of special mixed greens.

8   ounces packaged dried
    fettuccine

12 ounces skinless,
    boneless chicken
    breast halves

    Nonstick spray coating

1½ cups broccoli flowerets

1   medium red and/or
    yellow sweet pepper,
    cut into ¾-inch pieces

½   cup chopped onion

1   tablespoon cooking oil

1   10¾-ounce can
    condensed cream of
    chicken soup

1   teaspoon dried basil,
    crushed

½   cup shredded cheddar
    cheese (2 ounces)

● Cook the pasta according to the directions on page 9. Drain the pasta; cover to keep warm.

● Meanwhile, cut chicken into bite-size strips. Spray a cold large skillet with nonstick spray coating. Preheat the skillet over medium heat. Stir-fry broccoli, sweet pepper, and onion in the hot skillet for 3 to 4 minutes or until just tender; remove from skillet. Add oil to the skillet. Add chicken; stir-fry for 3 to 4 minutes or until chicken is tender and no longer pink. Drain off fat.

● Add cream of chicken soup, basil, and ½ cup *water* to the skillet; mix thoroughly. Stir in the vegetable mixture. Bring to boiling; reduce heat. Add cheddar cheese; cook and stir until cheese is almost melted.

● Serve the sauce over the pasta. Garnish with red and yellow pepper slices and parsley sprigs, if desired. Makes 4 servings.

Note: Pictured on pages 10–11 over carrot fettuccine.

Chicken and Clam Sauce

Per serving:
510 cal. (23% from fat), 36 g pro., 59 g carbo., 13 g fat,
111 mg cholesterol, 2 g dietary fiber, 465 mg sodium.

**Preparation time:
25 minutes**

Chicken, basil, and white wine give this clam sauce a delicious new twist. Serve it over plain or spinach linguine or fettuccine.

8   ounces packaged dried
    linguine or fettuccine

    Nonstick spray coating

8   ounces ground raw
    chicken or turkey

½   cup chopped onion

2   cloves garlic, minced

½   teaspoon dried basil,
    crushed

¼   cup all-purpose flour

1¼ cups chicken broth

¾   cup evaporated milk

1   10-ounce can whole
    baby clams, drained

¼   cup snipped parsley

¼   cup dry white wine or
    chicken broth

● Cook the pasta according to the directions on page 9. Drain the pasta; cover to keep warm.

● Meanwhile, spray a cold large saucepan with nonstick spray coating. Cook chicken or turkey, onion, garlic, basil, ⅛ teaspoon *salt*, and ⅛ teaspoon *pepper* in the saucepan until the chicken no longer is pink and the onion is tender.

● Stir flour into saucepan. Add chicken broth and milk. Cook and stir until thickened and bubbly. Cook and stir for 1 minute more. Stir in clams, parsley, and white wine; heat through.

● Serve the sauce over pasta. Makes 4 servings.

Meat and Fresh Vegetable Sauce

Per serving:
393 cal. (19% from fat), 23 g pro., 59 g carbo., 8 g fat,
42 mg cholesterol, 4 g dietary fiber, 548 mg sodium.

**Preparation time:
25 minutes**

**Cooking time:
30 minutes**

This all-purpose spaghetti sauce is bursting with vegetables. Keep some on hand in the freezer for use in lasagna or to serve over spaghetti for a deliciously quick meal.

- 8 ounces ground beef
- 1 cup sliced fresh mushrooms
- ½ cup chopped onion
- ½ cup chopped carrot
- ½ cup chopped green pepper
- ¼ cup chopped celery
- 1 clove garlic, minced
- 1 16-ounce can tomatoes
- ⅓ cup tomato paste
- ¼ cup water
- 1 small bay leaf
- ½ teaspoon dried basil, crushed
- ¼ teaspoon salt
- ¼ teaspoon dried oregano, crushed
- ⅛ teaspoon ground black pepper
- 8 ounces packaged dried spaghetti
- 1 tablespoon cold water
- 1 teaspoon cornstarch

- Cook meat, mushrooms, onion, carrot, green pepper, celery, and garlic in a large saucepan until meat is brown. Drain off fat.

- Cut up tomatoes. Stir *undrained* tomatoes, tomato paste, ¼ cup water, bay leaf, basil, salt, oregano, and black pepper into saucepan. Bring to boiling; reduce heat. Cover and simmer for 30 minutes, stirring occasionally.

- Meanwhile, cook the pasta according to the directions on page 9. Drain the pasta; cover to keep warm.

- Combine 1 tablespoon cold water and the cornstarch in a small bowl. Stir into sauce. Cook and stir until thickened and bubbly. Cook and stir for 2 minutes more.

- Discard the bay leaf. Serve the meat sauce over pasta. Makes 4 servings.

Start with Antipasto

Serving pasta at your next dinner party? Start the meal with an attractive antipasto tray as an appetizer. To assemble the tray, choose one or two of your favorite cold cuts, such as salami or ham. Then, add cheese cubes or slices, green or ripe olives, pickled peppers, marinated artichoke hearts, and/or fresh vegetable sticks. If you like, add a fruit, such as cantaloupe balls, honeydew melon slices, or strawberries, to complement the savory foods. Round out your pasta meal with a crusty bread, breadsticks, or crackers, and wine or sparkling water.

Creamy Tomato and Meat Sauce

Per serving:
541 cal. (37% from fat), 28 g pro., 57 g carbo., 22 g fat,
116 mg cholesterol, 2 g dietary fiber, 696 mg sodium.

Preparation time:
20 minutes

Whipping cream and Italian seasoning make this delicate sauce simply superb.

8	ounces packaged dried fusilli or vermicelli
12	ounces ground beef
1	cup chopped onion
2	cloves garlic, minced
1	14½-ounce can Italian-style stewed tomatoes
1	teaspoon dried Italian seasoning, crushed
½	teaspoon salt
⅛	teaspoon pepper
3	tablespoons cold water
4	teaspoons cornstarch
½	cup whipping cream
2	tablespoons snipped parsley

- Cook the pasta according to the directions on page 9. Drain the pasta; cover to keep warm.

- Meanwhile, for sauce, cook meat, onion, and garlic in a large saucepan until meat is brown. Drain off fat.

- Stir *undrained* stewed tomatoes, Italian seasoning, salt, and pepper into saucepan. Bring to boiling; reduce heat. Cover and simmer for 5 minutes, stirring occasionally.

- Combine cold water and cornstarch in a small bowl. Stir into tomato mixture. Cook and stir until thickened and bubbly. Cook and stir for 2 minutes more.

- Gradually stir whipping cream into the sauce. Heat through, stirring constantly. Remove from heat. Stir in snipped parsley.

- Serve the sauce over pasta. Garnish with rosemary sprigs, if desired. Makes 4 servings.

Marinara Sauce

Per serving:
428 cal. (15% from fat), 28 g pro., 63 g carbo., 7 g fat,
45 mg cholesterol, 6 g dietary fiber, 607 mg sodium.

Preparation time:
25 minutes

Cooking time:
30 minutes

Besides tricolor or regular corkscrew macaroni, this chunky tomato sauce is delicious with rigatoni, ziti, and medium shells.

1	cup chopped onion
2	large cloves garlic, minced
1	tablespoon olive oil
1	28-ounce can tomatoes, cut up
2	tablespoons tomato paste
1	teaspoon sugar
1	teaspoon dried Italian seasoning, crushed
¼	teaspoon salt
8	ounces packaged dried corkscrew macaroni
1½	cups chopped cooked chicken or fully cooked ham
1	cup frozen peas, frozen whole-kernel corn, and/or drained canned sliced mushrooms

- For sauce, cook onion and garlic in hot oil in a medium saucepan until onion is tender but not brown. Drain off fat. Stir in *undrained* tomatoes, tomato paste, sugar, Italian seasoning, salt, and dash *pepper*. Bring to boiling. Reduce heat; simmer, uncovered, about 30 minutes or until sauce is desired consistency, stirring occasionally.

- Meanwhile, cook the pasta according to the directions on page 9. Drain the pasta; cover to keep warm.

- Stir chicken or ham and vegetables into the saucepan and heat sauce through.

- Serve the sauce over pasta. Garnish with parsley, basil, or rosemary sprigs and cherry tomatoes, if desired. Makes 4 servings.

Marinara Sauce over tricolor corkscrew macaroni

15

Broccoli-Bacon Sauce

Per serving:
521 cal. (27% from fat), 25 g pro., 72 g carbo., 16 g fat,
58 mg cholesterol, 7 g dietary fiber, 938 mg sodium.

**Preparation time:
30 minutes**

Parsnip, broccoli, and Canadian-style bacon are flavorful additions to this easy sauce.

8	ounces packaged dried wagon wheels
1	large parsnip
1	small onion, sliced
2	cups broccoli flowerets
½	cup sliced celery
6	ounces thinly sliced Canadian-style bacon
4	ounces cream cheese
¾	cup milk
2	teaspoons cornstarch
⅛	teaspoon ground nutmeg
1	4½-ounce jar sliced mushrooms, drained
2	tablespoons grated Parmesan cheese

- Cook the pasta according to the directions on page 9. Drain the pasta; cover to keep warm.

- Meanwhile, cut parsnip into thin strips (strips should measure about 3 cups). Separate onion into rings. Cook parsnip, onion, broccoli, and celery in a small amount of boiling water in a covered saucepan for 7 to 9 minutes or until vegetables are crisp-tender. Drain vegetables and set aside.

- Chop Canadian-style bacon and cut cream cheese into cubes. Stir together milk, cornstarch, and nutmeg in the same saucepan used to cook vegetables. Stir in cream cheese. Cook and stir over medium heat until thickened and bubbly and cheese is melted. Stir in cooked vegetables, Canadian-style bacon, and mushrooms. Cook and stir for 2 minutes more or until heated through.

- Serve the sauce over pasta. Sprinkle with Parmesan cheese. Makes 4 servings.

Creamy Ham Sauce

Per serving:
411 cal. (26% from fat), 22 g pro., 54 g carbo., 12 g fat,
42 mg cholesterol, 2 g dietary fiber, 1,020 mg sodium.

**Preparation time:
20 minutes**

Chunks of ham, peas, and sliced mushrooms dress up this simple sauce based on cheddar cheese soup and sour cream.

12	ounces packaged dried medium shells
1	cup frozen peas
¼	cup chopped onion
1½	cups cubed fully cooked ham
1	10¾-ounce can condensed cheddar cheese soup
½	cup dairy sour cream
1	4½-ounce jar sliced mushrooms, drained
¼	cup milk
¼	cup shredded carrot
1	teaspoon dried oregano or basil, crushed
¼	teaspoon pepper
2	tablespoons grated Parmesan cheese

- Cook the pasta according to the directions on page 9, adding frozen peas and chopped onion during the last 6 minutes of cooking time. Drain the pasta mixture; cover to keep warm.

- Meanwhile, for sauce, stir together ham, cheddar cheese soup, sour cream, mushrooms, milk, carrot, oregano or basil, and pepper in a medium saucepan. Cook and stir over medium heat until heated through.

- Serve sauce over the pasta mixture. Sprinkle with Parmesan cheese. Makes 6 servings.

Rich Sausage and Mushroom Sauce

Per serving:
811 cal. (57% from fat), 27 g pro., 60 g carbo., 52 g fat,
176 mg cholesterol, 2 g dietary fiber, 796 mg sodium.

**Preparation time:
25 minutes**

This magnificent mostaccioli topper pairs a cream sauce with Italian sausage, and tastes every bit as rich as it does spicy.

8   ounces packaged dried mostaccioli

12 ounces bulk Italian sausage

2   cups sliced fresh shiitake or button mushrooms

1   small red or green sweet pepper, cut into bite-size pieces

½   cup chopped onion

1   clove garlic, minced

1½ cups whipping cream

2   tablespoons fresh snipped basil or 2 teaspoons dried basil, crushed

¼   teaspoon ground black pepper

½   cup grated Parmesan cheese

Basil leaves (optional)

- Cook the pasta according to the directions on page 9. Drain the pasta; cover to keep warm.

- Meanwhile, for sauce, cook sausage, mushrooms, red or green sweet pepper, onion, and garlic in a large skillet until the sausage is brown. Drain off fat.

- Stir whipping cream, basil, and black pepper into sausage mixture. Cook over medium-low heat for 5 to 8 minutes or until slightly thickened, stirring occasionally. Remove from heat. Stir in the Parmesan cheese.

- Serve the sauce over pasta. Garnish with basil leaves, if desired. Makes 4 servings.

Choose the Right Pasta

Enhance the flavor and appearance of sauces by teaming them with the right pasta. Here is a simple rule of thumb. Match a delicate sauce with a delicate pasta and a heavy sauce with a sturdy pasta. For example, pair a light vegetable sauce with angel hair pasta and a rich meat sauce with mostaccioli.

Also, keep ease of eating in mind when you choose a pasta. Long strands of spaghetti or fettuccine, for instance, can be twirled on a fork more easily if they are served with sauces that have small pieces, such as minced clams or crumbled ground beef. And sauces with larger chunks of meat or vegetables work well with shorter pastas, such as corkscrew macaroni or rigatoni, that you can scoop up with a fork. Smooth tomato or cheese sauces are great with just about any kind of pasta.

Vegetable-Garlic Sauce over spinach linguine

Vegetable-Garlic Sauce

Per serving:
392 cal. (24% from fat), 17 g pro., 58 g carbo., 11 g fat,
42 mg cholesterol, 2 g dietary fiber, 222 mg sodium.

**Preparation time:
20 minutes**

The rich colors and flavors of summer star in this simple, yet elegant entrée. Summer squash, sweet pepper, and leek brighten a creamy basil sauce.

8   ounces packaged dried linguine or fettuccine

1   medium yellow summer squash or zucchini

½   cup chopped red sweet pepper

½   cup thinly sliced leek

3   cloves garlic, minced

1   teaspoon margarine or butter

1   12-ounce can evaporated milk

1   tablespoon all-purpose flour

¼   teaspoon dried basil, crushed

¼   cup finely shredded Parmesan cheese

- Cook the pasta according to the directions on page 9. Drain the pasta; cover to keep warm.

- Meanwhile, for sauce, thinly slice yellow squash or zucchini. Cook squash, sweet pepper, and leek in a small amount of boiling water in a medium saucepan for 2 minutes. Drain vegetables and set aside.

- In the same saucepan used to cook vegetables, cook garlic in margarine or butter for 30 seconds. Add evaporated milk, flour, basil, and ⅛ teaspoon *ground black pepper* to the Tupperware® Quick Shake® container. Apply seal and cap; shake well. Add mixture to garlic in the saucepan.

- Cook and stir over medium heat until mixture is thickened and bubbly. Cook and stir for 1 minute more. Return vegetables to saucepan. Stir in the Parmesan cheese. Heat through.

- Serve the sauce over pasta. Sprinkle with additional freshly grated Parmesan cheese, if desired. Serves 4.

Creamy White Clam Sauce

Per serving:
491 cal. (30% from fat), 26 g pro., 57 g carbo., 17 g fat,
60 mg cholesterol, 1 g dietary fiber, 477 mg sodium.

**Preparation time:
20 minutes**

Ladle this sensational clam and wine sauce over spinach linguine for a colorful dinner presentation.

8   ounces packaged dried linguine or spaghetti

2   6½-ounce cans minced clams

     Half-and-half, light cream, or milk

½   cup chopped onion

2   cloves garlic, minced

2   tablespoons margarine or butter

¼   cup all-purpose flour

¼   teaspoon dried basil, crushed

¼   cup snipped parsley

¼   cup dry white wine or chicken broth

¼   cup grated Parmesan cheese

- Cook the pasta according to the directions on page 9. Drain the pasta; cover to keep warm.

- Meanwhile, drain clams, reserving liquid. Add enough half-and-half or light cream to the reserved liquid to make 1¾ cups.

- For sauce, cook onion and garlic in margarine or butter in a medium saucepan until onion is tender but not brown. Stir in flour, basil, ¼ teaspoon *salt,* and ⅛ teaspoon *pepper.* Add the half-and-half mixture all at once. Cook and stir until thickened and bubbly. Cook and stir for 1 minute more. Stir in parsley, wine, and clams. Heat through.

- Serve the sauce over pasta. Sprinkle with Parmesan cheese. Makes 4 servings.

Smoked Salmon Cream Sauce

Per serving:
509 cal. (51% from fat), 18 g pro., 45 g carbo., 29 g fat,
106 mg cholesterol, 1 g dietary fiber, 442 mg sodium.

Preparation time:
25 minutes

Lox-style salmon adds a
pleasant smoked flavor
that makes this cream
sauce irresistible.

8 ounces packaged dried
  linguine or fettuccine

6 ounces thinly sliced
  smoked salmon
  (lox-style)

¼ cup sliced green onions

1 clove garlic, minced

1 tablespoon margarine
  or butter

1 cup whipping cream

1 tablespoon fresh
  snipped dill or 1
  teaspoon dried dillweed

1 teaspoon finely
  shredded lemon peel

¼ teaspoon pepper

2 tablespoons grated
  Parmesan cheese

- Cook the pasta according to the directions on page 9. Drain the pasta; cover to keep warm.

- Meanwhile, cut the salmon into bite-size strips; set aside. For sauce, cook green onions and garlic in margarine or butter in a large skillet until tender. Add salmon and cook for 1 minute.

- Stir whipping cream, snipped dill, lemon peel, and pepper into skillet. Bring to boiling; reduce heat. Boil gently about 5 minutes or until the sauce thickens slightly. Remove from the heat. Stir in Parmesan cheese.

- Serve the sauce over pasta. Garnish with dill sprigs, if desired. Makes 4 servings.

Tomato-Tuna Sauce

Per serving:
435 cal. (15% from fat), 31 g pro., 63 g carbo., 7 g fat,
23 mg cholesterol, 5 g dietary fiber, 1,124 mg sodium.

Preparation time:
20 minutes

Cooking time:
20 minutes

Ground red pepper puts
some zing into this
Mediterranean-style sauce.

⅓ cup chopped onion

2 cloves garlic, minced

1 tablespoon olive oil

1 28-ounce can tomatoes

1 6-ounce can tomato
  paste

1 3½-ounce can pitted
  ripe olives, drained

1 teaspoon sugar

¾ teaspoon dried Italian
  seasoning, crushed

⅛ teaspoon salt

⅛ teaspoon ground red
  pepper

1 12½-ounce can tuna
  (water pack)

8 ounces packaged dried
  mostaccioli or rigatoni

- Cook onion and garlic in hot olive oil in a large saucepan until onion is tender but not brown. Drain fat.

- Finely cut up tomatoes. Carefully stir *undrained* tomatoes, tomato paste, ripe olives, sugar, Italian seasoning, salt, and ground red pepper into saucepan. Bring to boiling; reduce heat. Boil gently, uncovered, about 20 minutes or until sauce is desired consistency.

- Drain tuna and break into chunks. Stir tuna into tomato mixture and heat through.

- Meanwhile, cook the pasta according to the directions on page 9. Drain the pasta; return to the pan. Add the sauce and toss gently until pasta is coated. Transfer to a warm serving dish. Sprinkle with snipped parsley, if desired. Makes 4 servings.

Hot 'n' Spicy Sauce

Per serving:
482 cal. (30% from fat), 23 g pro., 63 g carbo., 16 g fat,
44 mg cholesterol, 5 g dietary fiber, 1,452 mg sodium.

Preparation time:
15 minutes

Cooking time:
40 minutes

The spicier the sausage, the more this recipe lives up to its name.

12 ounces bulk Italian sausage

½ cup chopped onion

¼ cup finely chopped green pepper

2 cloves garlic, minced

1 28-ounce can tomatoes, cut up

1 6-ounce can tomato paste

½ teaspoon salt

½ teaspoon dried oregano, crushed

½ teaspoon dried basil, crushed

¼ teaspoon ground black pepper

¼ teaspoon ground red pepper

8 ounces packaged dried spaghetti or fusilli

- Cook sausage, onion, green pepper, and garlic in a large saucepan until sausage is brown. Drain off fat.

- Stir *undrained* tomatoes, tomato paste, salt, oregano, basil, black pepper, and red pepper into saucepan. Bring to boiling; reduce heat. Cover; simmer for 30 minutes. Uncover; simmer for 10 to 15 minutes more or until sauce is desired consistency, stirring occasionally.

- Meanwhile, cook the pasta according to the directions on page 9. Drain the pasta.

- Serve the sauce over pasta. Makes 4 servings.

Pasta Protocol

The question of the proper way to eat long, slender pasta is open for debate. Some pasta pros insist you have to wind it on a fork. Here are two ways. Hook a few strands on the fork, rest the tines against a large spoon, and twirl to twist the pasta onto the fork. Or, rest the tip of fork on your plate, then wind the pasta onto the fork. Other pasta lovers, however, say forget the winding and just cut pasta into bite-size portions with a fork. Either way, when topped with one of the sauces in this section, the pasta is sure to taste great.

Best Beer-Cheese Sauce

Per serving:
379 cal. (22% from fat), 16 g pro., 56 g carbo., 9 g fat,
39 mg cholesterol, 3 g dietary fiber, 193 mg sodium.

Preparation time:
25 minutes

What makes this blend of sharp cheddar cheese and beer better than other cheese sauces? Carrots, zucchini, and mushrooms.

8	ounces packaged dried fettuccine
1	cup bias-sliced carrots
1	cup chopped zucchini
1	cup whole fresh mushrooms, quartered
1	cup milk
3	tablespoons all-purpose flour
¼	cup beer or chicken broth
¾	cup shredded sharp cheddar cheese (3 ounces)

• Cook the pasta according to the directions on page 9. Drain the pasta; cover to keep warm.

• Meanwhile, cook carrots in a small amount of boiling water in a covered medium saucepan for 6 minutes. Add zucchini and mushrooms. Cover and cook for 2 to 3 minutes more or until vegetables are crisp-tender. Drain the vegetables; keep warm.

• Add milk and flour to the Tupperware® Quick Shake® container. Apply seal and cap; shake well. Add mixture to the saucepan. Cook and stir over medium heat until thickened and bubbly. Add beer or broth; heat through.

• Remove pan from heat. Stir in cheddar cheese until just melted. Stir cooked vegetables into cheese sauce. Season to taste with salt and pepper, if desired. Serve the sauce over pasta. Makes 4 servings.

Garden Vegetable Sauce

Per serving:
290 cal. (35% from fat), 16 g pro., 32 g carbo., 12 g fat,
125 mg cholesterol, 5 g dietary fiber, 913 mg sodium.

Preparation time:
30 minutes

Cooking time:
45 minutes

For the same great taste with a different look, try this sage-seasoned sauce over cheese-filled ravioli.

½	cup chopped onion
½	cup sliced celery
2	cloves garlic, minced
1	tablespoon margarine or butter
1	28-ounce can tomatoes, cut up
1	cup sliced fresh mushrooms
½	cup chopped green pepper
1	tablespoon fresh snipped sage or 1 teaspoon dried sage, crushed
½	teaspoon sugar
¼	teaspoon salt
⅛	teaspoon ground black pepper
1	small yellow summer squash or zucchini
1	7-ounce package dried cheese tortellini

• For sauce, cook onion, celery, and garlic in margarine or butter in a large saucepan until tender. Stir in *undrained* tomatoes, mushrooms, green pepper, sage, sugar, salt, and ground black pepper. Bring to boiling; reduce heat. Simmer, uncovered, for 40 minutes.

• Cut summer squash or zucchini into ½-inch pieces. Add to sauce. Cook about 5 minutes more or until sauce is desired consistency and squash is tender.

• Meanwhile, cook the pasta according to the directions on page 9. Drain the pasta.

• To serve, toss the pasta and sauce gently until pasta is coated. Makes 4 servings.

Two-Bean Tomato Sauce

Per serving:
478 cal. (17% from fat), 22 g pro., 78 g carbo., 9 g fat,
32 mg cholesterol, 11 g dietary fiber, 805 mg sodium.

Preparation time:
15 minutes

Cooking time:
30 minutes

Kidney and garbanzo beans make this flavorful meatless sauce stick-to-the-ribs satisfying.

1   16-ounce can tomatoes

1½ cups water

1   cup chopped onion

1   6-ounce can tomato paste

2   cloves garlic, minced

1   teaspoon sugar

1   teaspoon instant beef bouillon granules

1   teaspoon dried oregano, crushed

½   teaspoon dried basil, crushed

⅛   teaspoon ground red pepper

⅛   teaspoon ground black pepper

12   ounces packaged dried linguine or fettuccine

1   15-ounce can red kidney beans

1   15-ounce can garbanzo beans

¼   cup snipped parsley

1   cup shredded cheddar cheese (4 ounces)

- For sauce, cut up tomatoes. Combine *undrained* tomatoes, water, onion, tomato paste, garlic, sugar, bouillon granules, oregano, basil, red pepper, and black pepper in a large saucepan. Bring to boiling; reduce heat. Simmer, uncovered, for 30 minutes.

- Meanwhile, cook the pasta according to the directions on page 9. Drain the pasta; cover to keep warm.

- Rinse and drain kidney beans and garbanzo beans. Slightly mash *half* of the kidney beans with a fork or potato masher in a medium mixing bowl. Add mashed and whole kidney beans and garbanzo beans to the sauce. Heat through. Stir in parsley.

- Serve the sauce over pasta. Sprinkle with cheddar cheese. Makes 6 servings.

Using Homemade Pasta

If you enjoy making your own homemade pasta (see recipe, page 8) or prefer to serve packaged refrigerated pasta, you can substitute either type for the packaged dried pasta called for in the recipes in this book. Just use twice as much homemade or refrigerated pasta as packaged dried pasta called for in a recipe.

Marvelous Main Dishes

Satisfy your passion for pasta! Simply choose any of these fabulous entrées, including flavorful casseroles, easy toss-togethers, and streamlined versions of traditional favorites. Whether you serve them for lunch or for dinner, you'll create sensational meals in minutes.

Cheese-Stuffed Manicotti
(See recipe, page 57.)

Beef Strips with Vermicelli

Per serving:
396 cal. (17% from fat), 25 g pro., 59 g carbo., 8 g fat,
37 mg cholesterol, 5 g dietary fiber, 543 mg sodium.

**Preparation time:
25 minutes**

A rich tomato sauce accents the tender beef, delicate green beans, and al dente vermicelli. Serve this with a fresh fruit salad for an easy weekday supper.

8	ounces packaged dried vermicelli or spaghetti
8	ounces boneless beef top round steak
½	cup chopped onion
1	tablespoon cooking oil
1	16-ounce can tomato wedges
1	9-ounce package frozen Italian-style or cut green beans
1	4½-ounce jar sliced mushrooms, drained
⅓	cup Italian-style tomato paste
¼	teaspoon pepper
1	tablespoon grated Parmesan cheese

- Cook the pasta according to the directions on page 9. Drain the pasta; cover to keep warm.

- Meanwhile, thinly slice meat into bite-size strips. Cook meat and onion in hot oil in a large skillet over medium-high heat until the meat is brown and onion is tender. Drain off fat.

- Stir *undrained* tomato wedges, green beans, mushrooms, tomato paste, and pepper into the skillet. Bring to boiling; reduce heat. Simmer, uncovered, for 7 to 8 minutes or until slightly thickened, stirring frequently. Stir in 1 tablespoon Parmesan cheese.

- Serve the beef-vegetable mixture over pasta. Sprinkle with additional grated Parmesan cheese, if desired. Makes 4 servings.

One-Pot Goulash

Per serving:
511 cal. (39% from fat), 37 g pro., 42 g carbo., 22 g fat,
153 mg cholesterol, 4 g dietary fiber, 556 mg sodium.

**Preparation time:
25 minutes**

**Cooking time:
15 minutes**

Choose domestic paprika to give this goulash a slightly sweet taste, or imported Hungarian paprika for a more pungent flavor.

1	pound boneless beef round steak
1	tablespoon cooking oil
½	cup chopped onion
1	clove garlic, minced
1	28-ounce can tomatoes
1	cup water
1	tablespoon paprika
½	teaspoon dried thyme, crushed
¼	teaspoon salt
¼	teaspoon pepper
5	ounces packaged dried medium noodles*
2	tablespoons all-purpose flour
1	8-ounce carton dairy sour cream

- Thinly slice meat into bite-size strips. Cook *half* of the meat in hot oil in a large saucepan until brown; remove meat from saucepan. Cook the remaining meat, onion, and garlic in saucepan until meat is brown and onion is tender. Drain off fat. Return all the meat to saucepan.

- Cut up tomatoes. Stir *undrained* tomatoes, water, paprika, thyme, salt, and pepper into saucepan. Bring to boiling. Add the *uncooked* pasta, a few pieces at a time, stirring constantly. Reduce heat; boil gently, uncovered, about 15 minutes or until meat and pasta are tender, stirring frequently.

- Stir the flour into the sour cream; stir into the meat and pasta mixture. Cook and stir until thickened and bubbly; cook and stir for 1 minute more. Makes 4 servings.

*Pasta should measure 2½ cups.

Beef-and-Noodle Stir-Fry

Per serving:
340 cal. (17% from fat), 32 g pro., 38 g carbo., 6 g fat,
72 mg cholesterol, 3 g dietary fiber, 1,000 mg sodium.

**Preparation time:
35 minutes**

Freshly grated gingerroot and sesame oil give this colorful dish an authentic Asian flavor. Accompany it with a citrus salad.

4 ounces packaged dried fettuccine

1 cup beef broth

2 tablespoons soy sauce

1 tablespoon cornstarch

1 teaspoon grated gingerroot or ¼ teaspoon ground ginger

Dash ground black pepper

1 medium yellow summer squash, halved lengthwise

1 teaspoon toasted sesame oil

1 small green pepper, cut into bite-size pieces

¼ cup sliced green onions

1 clove garlic, minced

8 ounces cooked beef, thinly sliced into bite-size pieces

1 cup quartered cherry tomatoes

Snipped cilantro or parsley

- Cook, rinse, and drain the pasta according to the directions on page 9.

- Meanwhile, for sauce, stir together beef broth, soy sauce, cornstarch, gingerroot, and black pepper in a small bowl. Set aside.

- Cut summer squash into ⅛-inch-thick slices. Heat ½ *teaspoon* of the sesame oil in a large nonstick skillet until hot. Stir-fry the squash, green pepper, green onions, and garlic in hot oil about 3 minutes or until squash is crisp-tender. Remove vegetables from skillet.

- Add the remaining oil to skillet. Stir-fry meat in hot oil until heated through. Push meat from the center of skillet. Stir the sauce; add to the center of the skillet. Cook and stir until thickened and bubbly. Cook and stir for 1 minute more.

- Add the cooked pasta, stir-fried vegetables, and cherry tomatoes to skillet. Stir to coat with sauce. Cook and lightly stir until heated through.

- To serve, transfer to a warm serving dish. Sprinkle with cilantro or parsley. Makes 3 or 4 servings.

Stir-Frying Made Simple

No matter how tight your schedule, you can have a delicious stir-fry on the table in minutes by taking the time to do a little early preparation. Up to 24 hours ahead of mealtime, prepare the meat, vegetables, and sauce as directed in the stir-fry recipe. Cover and refrigerate each ingredient in a separate Tupperware® refrigerator container. At mealtime, simply heat your wok or skillet and begin stir-frying.

Primavera Stroganoff Stir-Fry

Per serving:
531 cal. (35% from fat), 33 g pro., 54 g carbo., 21 g fat,
156 mg cholesterol, 1 g dietary fiber, 698 mg sodium.

**Preparation time:
25 minutes**

This simplified version of classic beef stroganoff uses purchased gravy for the sauce and quick-cooking frozen vegetables.

8 ounces packaged dried medium noodles

1 12-ounce jar brown or mushroom gravy

½ cup dairy sour cream

1 4½-ounce jar sliced mushrooms, drained

1 teaspoon dried dillweed

12 ounces boneless beef top round steak or pork

4 green onions

2 tablespoons cooking oil

2 cups loose-pack frozen zucchini, carrot, lima beans, cauliflower, and Italian beans

• Cook the pasta according to the directions on page 9. Drain the pasta; cover to keep warm.

• Meanwhile, for sauce, stir together gravy, sour cream, mushrooms, dillweed, ¼ teaspoon *salt*, and ¼ teaspoon *pepper*. Set aside.

• Thinly slice meat into bite-size strips. Bias-slice green onions into 1-inch lengths. Add *1 tablespoon* of the cooking oil to a wok or large skillet. Preheat over medium-high heat. Stir-fry frozen vegetables for 2 minutes. Add green onions and stir-fry about 2 minutes more or until the vegetables are tender. Remove the vegetables from the wok.

• Add the remaining oil to the wok. Add the meat. Stir-fry for 2 to 3 minutes or until done. Drain off fat. Push the meat from the center of the wok. Stir the sauce; add to the center of wok. Cook and stir until heated through. Return vegetables to the wok. Stir to coat with the sauce. Heat through. Serve over the pasta. Makes 4 servings.

Deep-Dish Pasta Pie

Per serving:
275 cal. (32% from fat), 20 g pro., 27 g carbo., 10 g fat,
76 mg cholesterol, 1 g dietary fiber, 509 mg sodium.

**Preparation time:
1 hour**

The corkscrew macaroni crust adds appeal to this hearty meat pie. Accompany this with a fresh greens salad.

5 ounces packaged dried corkscrew macaroni*

1 beaten egg

¼ cup milk

2 tablespoons grated Parmesan cheese

8 ounces ground beef

⅓ cup chopped onion

1 clove garlic, minced

1 14½-ounce can Italian-style stewed tomatoes

1 medium green and/or yellow sweet pepper

½ teaspoon dried Italian seasoning, crushed

1 4½-ounce jar sliced mushrooms, drained

¼ teaspoon crushed red pepper

1 cup shredded mozzarella cheese (4 ounces)

• Cook and drain the pasta according to the directions on page 9.

• For crust, combine egg, milk, and Parmesan cheese in a large mixing bowl. Stir in the pasta. Spread the pasta mixture evenly in a 9-inch quiche dish or pie plate. Bake, uncovered, in a 350° oven for 8 minutes.

• Meanwhile, cook meat, onion, and garlic in large skillet until the meat is brown. Drain off fat. Cut up tomatoes. Cut sweet pepper into 2-inch strips. Add *undrained* tomatoes, sweet pepper, and Italian seasoning to skillet. Bring to boiling; reduce heat. Simmer, uncovered, for 10 to 12 minutes or until peppers are just tender and most of the liquid is evaporated, stirring once or twice. Stir in mushrooms and crushed red pepper.

• Spoon the meat mixture over the pasta crust. Sprinkle with mozzarella cheese. Bake, uncovered, for 15 to 18 minutes more or until heated through and the cheese is melted. Makes 6 servings.

*Pasta should measure 2 cups.

Deep-Dish Pasta Pie

Beef and Vegetables with Bow Ties

Per serving:
361 cal. (35% from fat), 30 g pro., 30 g carbo., 14 g fat, 84 mg cholesterol, 7 g dietary fiber, 875 mg sodium.

Preparation time: 25 minutes

This stew, made with bow-tie pasta, will surprise diners with its delightful hint of cinnamon.

1   medium zucchini

1   9-ounce package frozen cut green beans

1   cup frozen sliced carrots

1½   ounces packaged dried bow ties (about ¾ cup)

1   medium onion

1   pound ground beef

1   15-ounce can herbed tomato sauce

1   4½-ounce jar sliced mushrooms, drained

¼   cup snipped dried tomatoes*

½   teaspoon ground cinnamon

½   teaspoon dried oregano, crushed

- Halve the zucchini lengthwise and cut into ½-inch slices. Cook green beans, carrots, and pasta according to the pasta-cooking directions on page 9, adding the zucchini during the last 3 minutes of cooking time. Drain the pasta mixture; cover to keep warm.

- Slice onion and separate it into rings. Cook meat and onion in a medium saucepan until meat is brown and onion is tender. Drain fat. Stir tomato sauce, mushrooms, tomatoes, cinnamon, oregano, ¼ cup *water*, ¼ teaspoon *salt*, and ¼ teaspoon *pepper* into meat mixture. Bring to boiling. Reduce heat. Cover and simmer 10 minutes.

- To serve, toss the meat mixture with pasta mixture. Makes 4 servings.

*Do not use oil-packed dried tomatoes.

Baked Mostaccioli with Meat Sauce

Per serving:
389 cal. (33% from fat), 28 g pro., 37 g carbo., 14 g fat, 66 mg cholesterol, 2 g dietary fiber, 612 mg sodium.

Preparation time: 30 minutes

Baking time: 20 minutes

Italian seasonings and green olives add character to the tomato-based sauce. Preparing this in individual casseroles keeps the baking time to a minimum.

8   ounces packaged dried mostaccioli or cavatelli

1   16-ounce can plum tomatoes

⅓   cup tomato paste

½   teaspoon sugar

½   teaspoon dried oregano, crushed

½   teaspoon dried thyme, crushed

¼   teaspoon pepper

1   pound ground beef

½   cup chopped onion

1   clove garlic, minced

½   cup sliced pimiento-stuffed green olives

1   cup shredded mozzarella cheese (4 ounces)

- Cook, rinse, and drain the pasta according to the directions on page 9.

- Meanwhile, combine *undrained* tomatoes, tomato paste, sugar, oregano, thyme, pepper, and ¼ cup *water* in a blender container or food processor bowl. Cover and blend or process until the mixture is smooth. Set aside.

- Cook meat, onion, and garlic in a large skillet until the meat is brown. Drain off fat. Stir in the tomato mixture. Bring to boiling; reduce heat. Cover and simmer for 10 minutes. Stir in the cooked pasta and the olives.

- Divide the pasta mixture among six 10-ounce casseroles. Bake, uncovered, in a 375° oven for 15 minutes. (*Or,* spoon all of the pasta mixture into a 2-quart casserole and bake, uncovered, for 30 minutes.) Sprinkle with mozzarella cheese. Bake about 5 minutes more or until heated through. Makes 6 servings.

Spaghetti Pie

Per serving:
442 cal. (41% from fat), 33 g pro., 32 g carbo., 20 g fat,
142 mg cholesterol, 2 g dietary fiber, 748 mg sodium.

**Preparation time:
35 minutes**

**Baking time:
25 minutes**

This layered meat dish will quickly become a family favorite. It features a spaghetti crust topped with layers of cheese and meat sauce.

6   ounces packaged dried spaghetti

2   tablespoons margarine or butter

2   well-beaten eggs

⅓   cup grated Parmesan cheese

1   pound ground beef or bulk pork sausage

½   cup chopped onion

¼   cup chopped green pepper

1   7½-ounce can tomatoes, cut up

1   6-ounce can tomato paste

1   teaspoon sugar

1   teaspoon dried oregano, crushed

¼   teaspoon garlic salt

1   cup cream-style cottage cheese (8 ounces), drained

½   cup shredded mozzarella cheese (2 ounces)

- Cook the pasta according to the directions on page 9. Drain the pasta; return to the pan. Stir margarine or butter into hot pasta. Stir in eggs and Parmesan cheese. Press pasta mixture into a buttered 10-inch pie plate, forming a crust.

- Cook meat, onion, and green pepper in a large skillet until meat is brown and vegetables are tender. Drain off fat. Stir in *undrained* tomatoes, tomato paste, sugar, oregano, and garlic salt. Heat through.

- Spread the cottage cheese over bottom of the prepared crust. Top with the meat mixture.

- Bake, uncovered, in a 350° oven for 20 minutes. Sprinkle with the mozzarella cheese. Bake about 5 minutes more or until cheese melts. Makes 6 servings.

Microwave Spaghetti Pie

Cut the baking time for Spaghetti Pie by using your microwave oven. First, cook the pasta and prepare the crust as directed in the recipe above. Cover the crust with waxed paper. Micro-cook on 50% power (medium) for 5 to 7 minutes or until just set, giving dish a half-turn once.

Meanwhile, prepare the meat mixture as directed in the recipe above. Spread the cottage cheese over bottom of the prepared crust. Top with the meat mixture. Cover with waxed paper. Cook on medium for 3 to 5 minutes or until heated through, giving the dish a half-turn once.

Finally, sprinkle with the shredded mozzarella cheese. Let stand for 5 minutes or until cheese melts.

Oriental Chicken Linguine
over beet linguine

Oriental
Chicken Linguine

Per serving:
424 cal. (23% from fat), 29 g pro., 51 g carbo., 11 g fat,
69 mg cholesterol, 3 g dietary fiber, 689 mg sodium.

**Preparation time:
25 minutes**

For a special dinner, serve
this colorful chicken-and-
vegetable combo over beet
linguine.

2   tablespoons soy sauce

2   tablespoons dry sherry
     or water

2   teaspoons cornstarch

12   ounces skinless,
     boneless chicken breast
     halves or thighs, cut
     into bite-size strips

8   ounces packaged dried
     linguine

1   tablespoon cooking oil

1   teaspoon toasted
     sesame oil

3   cups sliced fresh
     mushrooms

1   medium red and/or
     yellow sweet pepper,
     cut into 2-inch strips

1   6-ounce package frozen
     pea pods

½   cup water

½   teaspoon instant
     chicken bouillon
     granules

1   tablespoon toasted
     sesame seed

- For marinade, stir together soy sauce, dry sherry or
  water, and cornstarch in a medium bowl. Add the
  chicken; stir to coat. Set aside.

- Cook the pasta according to the directions on page 9.
  Drain the pasta; cover to keep warm.

- Meanwhile, add cooking oil and sesame oil to a wok or
  large skillet. Preheat over medium-high heat (add more
  cooking oil as necessary during cooking). Add
  mushrooms and sweet pepper to wok; stir-fry for 2
  minutes. Add frozen pea pods; stir-fry for 1 to 2 minutes
  more or until the vegetables are crisp-tender. Remove
  vegetables from wok; keep warm.

- Drain the chicken, reserving soy mixture. Stir-fry
  chicken in the hot wok for 2 to 3 minutes or until
  chicken is tender and no longer pink. Push the chicken
  from center of wok. Combine the water, bouillon
  granules, and reserved soy mixture; add to center of
  wok. Cook and stir until the mixture is slightly
  thickened and bubbly. Cook and stir 1 minute more.

- To serve, arrange the vegetables and chicken mixture
  over pasta on individual plates. Sprinkle each serving
  with sesame seed. Makes 4 servings.

Toasting Sesame Seed

Keep toasted sesame seeds on hand to add a rich, nutty flavor
to just about any stir-fry. To toast sesame seeds, spread them
in a thin layer in a shallow ungreased baking pan. Bake in
a 350° oven about 10 minutes or until golden, stirring once
or twice and checking often. Let seeds cool, then place in
a Tupperware® Freezer Mates® container. Freeze the toasted
seeds for up to six months.

Savory Almond Meatballs

Per serving:
539 cal. (40% from fat), 33 g pro., 48 g carbo., 24 g fat,
147 mg cholesterol, 2 g dietary fiber, 560 mg sodium.

Preparation time:
45 minutes

Impress family or friends with these almond-studded meatballs in a creamy pasta sauce. You can prepare the meatballs ahead and freeze them, if you like. Then defrost the meatballs overnight in the refrigerator and reheat in a skillet before adding to the sauce.

1	egg white
2	tablespoons milk
¼	teaspoon pepper
⅛	teaspoon dried thyme, crushed
½	cup finely chopped onion
⅓	cup finely crushed zwieback or fine dry bread crumbs
¼	cup chopped toasted almonds
¼	cup snipped parsley
1	pound ground beef or pork
2	tablespoons margarine or butter
8	ounces packaged dried medium noodles*
2	tablespoons all-purpose flour
2	teaspoons instant beef bouillon granules
⅛	teaspoon pepper
2	cups milk

- To make meatballs, combine egg white, the 2 tablespoons milk, ¼ teaspoon pepper, and thyme in a mixing bowl. Stir in onion, zwieback or bread crumbs, almonds, and parsley. Add the meat; mix well. Shape into 30 meatballs.

- Cook meatballs, half at a time, in margarine or butter in a large skillet over medium heat about 10 minutes or until no pink remains, turning often. Remove meatballs from skillet, reserving 2 tablespoons of the drippings in the skillet. Drain the meatballs on paper towels.

- Meanwhile, cook the pasta according to the directions on page 9. Drain the pasta; cover to keep warm.

- Stir flour, bouillon granules, and ⅛ teaspoon pepper into the reserved drippings in skillet. Add the 2 cups milk all at once. Cook and stir until thickened and bubbly. Cook and stir for 1 minute more. Return the meatballs to the skillet. Heat through.

- Serve meatball mixture over pasta. Makes 5 servings.

  *Pasta should measure about 4 cups.

Perfect Meatballs

To quickly shape even-sized meatballs, pat the meatball mixture into a log about 1½ inches in diameter. Then, cut the log into the same number of slices as number of meatballs specified in the recipe. Finally, using your hands, shape each slice into a round ball.

Spaghetti and Meatballs

Per serving:
402 cal. (11% from fat), 25 g pro., 67 g carbo., 5 g fat,
30 mg cholesterol, 5 g dietary fiber, 884 mg sodium.

**Preparation time:
1 hour 10 minutes**

Italian seasoning gives this sauce a zesty accent. What's more, it eliminates the work of measuring serveral herbs.

Mushroom Spaghetti Sauce (see recipe below right)

1 slightly beaten egg white

½ cup soft bread crumbs

2 tablespoons finely chopped onion

8 ounces lean ground beef

8 ounces packaged dried spaghetti

1 tablespoon cornstarch

1 tablespoon cold water

Grated Parmesan cheese (optional)

- Prepare Mushroom Spaghetti Sauce.

- Meanwhile, for meatballs, stir together egg white, bread crumbs, and the onion in a medium mixing bowl. Add the meat; mix well. Shape into 24 meatballs. Place in an 11x7x1½-inch baking pan.

- Bake, uncovered, in a 375° oven about 15 minutes or until no pink remains. Drain meatballs on paper towels. Add meatballs to Mushroom Spaghetti Sauce. Return sauce to boiling; reduce heat. Simmer meatball mixture, uncovered, for 10 minutes.

- Meanwhile, cook the pasta according to the directions on page 9. Drain the pasta; cover to keep warm.

- Combine cornstarch and cold water in a small bowl; stir into meatball mixture. Cook and stir until thickened and bubbly. Cook and stir for 2 minutes more.

- Serve the meatball mixture over pasta. Sprinkle with Parmesan cheese, if desired. Makes 4 servings.

Mushroom Spaghetti Sauce: Spray a 3-quart saucepan with *nonstick spray coating*. Preheat saucepan over medium heat. Add 1½ cups sliced *fresh mushrooms*, ½ cup chopped *onion*, ½ cup chopped *green pepper*, and 2 cloves *garlic*, minced. Cook and stir for 2 to 3 minutes or until onion is tender. Cut up tomatoes in two 14½-ounce cans *tomatoes*. Stir *undrained* tomatoes, one 8-ounce can *tomato sauce*, 1 tablespoon dried *Italian seasoning* (crushed), 1 teaspoon *sugar*, ¼ teaspoon *salt*, and 1 *bay leaf* into saucepan. Bring sauce to boiling; reduce heat. Cover and simmer sauce for 30 minutes. Discard bay leaf.

Pasta with a Twist

Add a delicious new twist to a favorite pasta recipe by using a specialty pasta in place of an ordinary one. You'll find dozens of options. Pick from whole-wheat pasta, colorful vegetable pastas such as spinach or carrot fettuccine and beet linguine, or herb-flavored pastas made with tarragon, oregano, rosemary, or another herb. If you like hot and spicy foods, look for black pepper pastas, pastas seasoned with chili peppers, or three-pepper pastas made with sweet pepper, coarsely ground or cracked black pepper, and ground red pepper. For festive dishes, use tricolor combinations, which usually include plain, green, and rosy versions of the same pasta.

Cincinnati-Style Chicken Chili

Per serving:
585 cal. (22% from fat), 35 g pro., 83 g carbo., 15 g fat,
95 mg cholesterol, 13 g dietary fiber, 1,029 mg sodium.

Preparation time:
20 minutes

Cooking time:
45 minutes

Ladle this rich, spicy chili over hot cooked pasta the way Cincinnati natives have for generations.

1   pound ground raw chicken

1   cup chopped onion

1   clove garlic, minced

3   tablespoons chili powder

2   teaspoons paprika

1   teaspoon ground cumin

½   teaspoon salt

½   teaspoon ground cinnamon

⅛   teaspoon ground cloves

⅛   teaspoon ground red pepper

1   14½-ounce can stewed tomatoes

1   8-ounce can tomato sauce

½   cup water

1   tablespoon red wine vinegar

1   tablespoon molasses

1   bay leaf

1   15-ounce can red kidney beans

8   ounces packaged dried spaghetti or linguine

¼   cup bias-sliced green onions

- Cook chicken, chopped onion, and garlic in a 4½-quart Dutch oven over medium heat for 5 to 7 minutes or until chicken no longer is pink. Drain off fat, if necessary.

- Add chili powder, paprika, cumin, salt, cinnamon, ground cloves, and red pepper to Dutch oven. Cook and stir over medium heat for 3 minutes. Stir in *undrained* stewed tomatoes, tomato sauce, water, vinegar, molasses and bay leaf. Bring to boiling; reduce heat. Cover and simmer for 45 minutes, stirring occasionally.

- Rinse and drain kidney beans. Stir into Dutch oven. Simmer the chicken mixture, uncovered, until desired consistency and kidney beans are heated through. Discard bay leaf.

- Meanwhile, cook the pasta according to the directions on page 9. Drain the pasta; cover to keep warm.

- Serve the chicken mixture over pasta. Sprinkle with bias-sliced green onions. Garnish with green onion fans, if desired. Makes 4 servings.

Get the Most from Garlic

To speed up your cooking, remember these tips when you work with garlic.

Garlic skin will come off more easily if you crush each clove with the flat side of a chef's knife before slipping off the skin.

Once each clove is peeled, mince it with a garlic press. Or, use a sharp knife to cut it into tiny pieces.

If you use a lot of garlic, consider purchasing commercially minced or chopped garlic. Substitute ½ teaspoon of bottled garlic for 1 fresh clove.

*Cincinnati-Style Chicken Chili
(single serving shown in a
Tupperware® 3-cup
Reheatables™ bowl)*

Bow Ties with Sausage and Peppers

Per serving:
386 cal. (37% from fat), 19 g pro., 43 g carbo., 16 g fat,
44 mg cholesterol, 2 g dietary fiber, 692 mg sodium.

**Preparation time:
30 minutes**

Because of its shape, rope macaroni (gemelli) is another good pasta choice for this spirited sausage and vegetable dish.

6 ounces packaged dried bow ties

1 large red sweet pepper

1 large green pepper

12 ounces mild or hot Italian sausage links

½ cup chopped onion

2 cloves garlic, minced

1 cup sliced fresh mushrooms

1 large tomato

⅔ cup chicken broth

2 teaspoons cornstarch

1 teaspoon dried basil, crushed

- Cook the pasta according to the directions on page 9. Drain the pasta; cover to keep warm.

- Meanwhile, cut red sweet pepper and green pepper into 1-inch pieces. Cut sausage links into ½-inch pieces. Cook the sausage, onion, and garlic in a large skillet for 5 minutes. Add red sweet pepper, green pepper, and mushrooms. Cook about 5 minutes more or until sausage is brown. Drain off fat.

- Coarsely chop tomato. Mix chicken broth, cornstarch, and basil in a small bowl. Add to the sausage mixture. Cook and stir until thickened and bubbly. Cook and stir for 2 minutes more. Stir in coarsely chopped tomato; heat through.

- To serve, toss the sausage mixture and pasta gently until pasta is coated. Makes 4 servings.

Skillet Taco Spaghetti

Per serving:
414 cal. (39% from fat), 28 g pro., 38 g carbo., 19 g fat,
76 mg cholesterol, 2 g dietary fiber, 1,223 mg sodium.

**Preparation time:
25 minutes**

To make this easy Tex-Mex dish even more special, accompany it with an assortment of toppings, such as guacamole, broken tortilla chips, shredded lettuce, chopped tomato, and sour cream.

5 ounces packaged dried wagon wheels*

1 pound ground beef

1 cup chopped onion

¾ cup water

2 tablespoons taco seasoning mix

1 11-ounce can whole-kernel corn with sweet peppers, drained

½ cup sliced pitted ripe olives

½ cup salsa

1 cup shredded cheddar cheese (4 ounces)

1 4-ounce can diced green chili peppers, drained

- Cook, rinse, and drain pasta according to directions on page 9.

- Cook meat and onion in a 12-inch skillet until meat is brown. Drain off fat. Stir in water and taco seasoning mix. Bring to boiling; reduce heat. Simmer, uncovered, for 2 minutes, stirring occasionally.

- Stir in cooked pasta, corn, olives, salsa, *half* of the shredded cheese, and the chili peppers. Heat through. Sprinkle with remaining cheese. Makes 6 servings.

*Pasta should measure 1⅔ cups.

Spicy Sausage Salad Toss

Per serving:
470 cal. (58% from fat), 24 g pro., 26 g carbo., 30 g fat,
77 mg cholesterol, 3 g dietary fiber, 1,617 mg sodium.

**Preparation time:
25 minutes**

This tortellini salad goes
south-of-the-border—
thanks to zesty salsa.

1 7-ounce package dried
    cheese tortellini

2 medium zucchini, cut
    into ½-inch slices

1 pound bulk pork
    sausage

4 green onions, bias-
    sliced into 1-inch
    pieces

1 cup chunky salsa

4 cups torn mixed salad
    greens

    Chunky salsa (optional)

- Cook pasta according to the directions on page 9, adding
  the zucchini during the last 5 minutes of cooking time.
  Drain pasta mixture; cover to keep warm.

- Meanwhile, cook sausage and green onions in a medium
  skillet until sausage is brown and onion is tender. Drain
  mixture well. Stir in 1 cup salsa. Heat mixture through.

- To serve, toss together pasta mixture, sausage mixture,
  and salad greens in a large salad bowl. If desired, serve
  with additional salsa. Makes 4 servings.

Cheese, Sausage, and Tortellini Toss

Per serving:
423 cal. (62% from fat), 22 g pro., 18 g carbo., 30 g fat,
71 mg cholesterol, 3 g dietary fiber, 1,066 mg sodium.

**Preparation time:
25 minutes**

Choose tricolor tortellini
for this Polish sausage
and Swiss cheese combo
when you want to give
it extra color.

½ of a 7-ounce package
    dried cheese tortellini
    (about 1 cup)

3 cups broccoli flowerets

8 ounces fully cooked
    smoked Polish sausage,
    halved lengthwise and
    thinly bias-sliced

1 tablespoon margarine
    or butter

1 tablespoon all-purpose
    flour

1 teaspoon caraway seed

1 cup milk

1 cup shredded process
    Swiss cheese (4 ounces)

1 tablespoon coarse-grain
    brown mustard

- Cook the pasta according to the directions on page 9,
  adding the broccoli and sausage during the last 5
  minutes of cooking time. Drain the pasta mixture; cover
  to keep warm.

- Meanwhile, melt the margarine or butter in a medium
  saucepan. Stir in flour and caraway seed. Add the milk
  all at once. Cook and stir until thickened and bubbly.
  Add the Swiss cheese and brown mustard, stirring until
  the cheese melts.

- To serve, toss the cheese mixture and pasta mixture
  gently until pasta is coated. Makes 4 servings.

*Beef-and-Mushroom-
Stuffed Shells*

Beef-and-Mushroom-Stuffed Shells

Per serving:
291 cal. (33% from fat), 23 g pro., 24 g carbo., 11 g fat,
63 mg cholesterol, 3 g dietary fiber, 572 mg sodium.

Preparation time:
30 minutes

Baking time:
20 minutes

A savory ground beef and vegetable mixture fills these jumbo shells, baked in a classic smooth tomato sauce. Try this attractive dish the next time you entertain.

8   packaged dried jumbo pasta shells

1   16-ounce can tomatoes, cut up

¼   cup dry red wine or water

2   tablespoons tomato paste

1   tablespoon cornstarch

½   teaspoon salt

½   teaspoon dried oregano, crushed

¼   teaspoon fennel seed, crushed

12 ounces ground beef

2   cups sliced fresh mushrooms

½   cup chopped onion

½   cup chopped green pepper

1   clove garlic, minced

¼   cup grated Parmesan cheese (optional)

Oregano sprigs (optional)

- Cook, rinse, and drain the pasta according to the directions on page 9.

- Meanwhile, combine *undrained* tomatoes, red wine or water, tomato paste, cornstarch, salt, dried oregano, and fennel seed in a saucepan. Cook and stir until thickened and bubbly. Remove from heat.

- Cook meat, mushrooms, onion, green pepper, and garlic in a large skillet until meat is brown. Drain off fat. Stir in *½ cup* of the tomato mixture.

- Spoon the meat mixture into pasta shells. Place in a 2-quart square baking dish. Pour the remaining tomato mixture over filled shells. Cover and bake in a 350° oven for 20 to 25 minutes or until heated through. Sprinkle with Parmesan cheese and garnish with oregano sprigs, if desired. Makes 4 servings.

Filling Jumbo Shells

With a little practice, you can stuff jumbo pasta shells perfectly every time. Start by cooking the shells so they are tender, but still firm. If you overcook them, they may tear as you stuff them. Drain the cooked shells in a colander, such as the Tupperware® Double Colander, then rinse them with cold running water. After rinsing the shells, turn each shell open side down to drain and place on waxed paper to keep the shells separate. To stuff the shells, work with one at a time. Cradle it gently in one hand and spoon in the filling. Use a small spoon so you can pack the shells with filling without tearing them.

Sausage Lasagna

Per serving:
464 cal. (44% from fat), 31 g pro., 35 g carbo., 23 g fat,
100 mg cholesterol. 3 g dietary fiber, 1,270 mg sodium.

Preparation time:
40 minutes

Baking time:
30 minutes

Standing time:
10 minutes

Accompany this luscious lasagna with a tossed spinach salad and some crispy breadsticks.

8   ounces bulk pork or Italian sausage

2   cups sliced fresh mushrooms

¾   cup chopped onion

½   cup chopped green pepper

2   cloves garlic, minced

1   8-ounce can tomato sauce

1   7½-ounce can tomatoes, cut up

1   6-ounce can tomato paste

1½ teaspoons dried basil, crushed

1   teaspoon dried oregano, crushed

6   packaged dried lasagna noodles

1½ cups ricotta cheese

1   beaten egg

½   cup grated Parmesan cheese

¼   teaspoon ground black pepper

1½ cups shredded mozzarella cheese (6 ounces)

- For meat sauce, cook sausage, mushrooms, onion, green pepper, and garlic in a large saucepan until the meat is brown and vegetables are tender. Drain off fat.

- Stir tomato sauce, *undrained* tomatoes, tomato paste, basil, and oregano into saucepan. Bring to boiling; reduce heat. Cover and simmer for 15 minutes, stirring occasionally.

- Meanwhile, cook, rinse, and drain the pasta according to the directions on page 9.

- For filling, drain the ricotta cheese. Stir together the ricotta, egg, *¼ cup* of the Parmesan cheese, and the ground black pepper.

- Layer *half* of the cooked noodles in a 2-quart rectangular baking dish. Spread with *half* of the filling. Top with *half* of the meat sauce and *half* of the mozzarella cheese. Repeat layers. Sprinkle with remaining Parmesan cheese.

- Bake in a 375° oven for 30 to 35 minutes or until heated through. Let lasagna stand 10 minutes before serving. Makes 6 to 8 servings.

Layering Lasagna

Layer lasagna like a pro—just follow these simple tips.

To keep cooked lasagna noodles from sticking together, drain the noodles in a colander, such as the Tupperware® Double Colander. Rinse with cold water, then put the noodles in a single layer on waxed paper.

Place the noodles in the baking dish, trimming them with kitchen scissors or a knife so they fit exactly in the dish. Be sure to overlap the noodles slightly to keep the sauce or filling from oozing out between the noodles.

Ham and Pasta with Mushrooms

Per serving:
411 cal. (33% from fat), 24 g pro., 44 g carbo., 15 g fat,
53 mg cholesterol, 3 g dietary fiber, 760 mg sodium.

**Preparation time:
25 minutes**

Choose spinach linguine for added color in this quick, mouthwatering supper.

2   medium carrots

6   ounces packaged dried linguine

1   cup broccoli flowerets

6   ounces sliced fully cooked ham

1   cup sliced fresh mushrooms

2   tablespoons margarine or butter

2   tablespoons all-purpose flour

1   tablespoon snipped parsley

½   teaspoon dried basil, crushed

1¼   cups milk

½   cup shredded cheddar cheese (2 ounces)

- Cut the carrots into ½-inch pieces. Cook the carrots and pasta according to the pasta-cooking directions on page 9, adding the broccoli during the last 3 to 5 minutes of cooking time. Drain pasta mixture; cover to keep warm.

- Meanwhile, cut the ham into bite-size strips. Cook mushrooms in margarine or butter in a medium saucepan until tender. Stir in flour, parsley, and basil. Add milk all at once. Cook and stir until thickened and bubbly. Add ham and cheddar cheese, stirring until the cheese melts.

- To serve, toss the ham mixture and pasta gently until pasta is coated. Makes 4 servings.

Chicken Paprika

Per serving:
646 cal. (46% from fat), 34 g pro., 55 g carbo., 33 g fat,
177 mg cholesterol, 2 g dietary fiber, 729 mg sodium.

**Preparation time:
25 minutes**

A traditional blend of seasonings and vegetables gives this easy chicken dish exceptional flavor.

8   ounces packaged dried wide noodles (4 cups)

3   cups sliced fresh mushrooms

½   cup chopped onion

2   cloves garlic, minced

¼   cup margarine or butter

2   to 3 teaspoons paprika

¼   teaspoon pepper

2   cups cubed cooked chicken

1   14½-ounce can chicken broth

2   tablespoons tomato paste

1   8-ounce carton dairy sour cream

3   tablespoons all-purpose flour

- Cook the pasta according to the directions on page 9. Drain the pasta; cover to keep warm.

- Meanwhile, cook mushrooms, onion, and garlic in margarine or butter in a large skillet over medium heat about 5 minutes or until the vegetables are tender. Stir in paprika and pepper. Cook and stir for 1 minute more. Stir in cooked chicken, chicken broth, and tomato paste. Bring to boiling.

- Stir together sour cream and flour. Stir into the chicken mixture. Cook and stir until thickened and bubbly. Cook and stir for 1 minute more.

- Serve the chicken mixture over pasta. Garnish with snipped parsley, if desired. Makes 4 servings.

Red Pepper Pasta Primavera

Per serving:
559 cal. (43% from fat), 28 g pro., 52 g carbo., 27 g fat,
79 mg cholesterol, 4 g dietary fiber, 543 mg sodium.

**Preparation time:
30 minutes**

Toss together a rainbow of
vegetables, fettuccine,
chicken, and a refreshingly
light pesto for this
company-special dish.

1 cup fresh snipped basil

1 medium red or green
sweet pepper, cut up

½ cup mayonnaise

2 tablespoons grated
Parmesan cheese

1 tablespoon lemon juice

½ teaspoon salt

⅛ teaspoon ground red
pepper

⅛ teaspoon ground black
pepper

8 ounces packaged dried
fettuccine

2 large carrots, cut into
thin strips

1 medium onion, cut into
thin wedges

1 medium zucchini
and/or yellow summer
squash, cut into thin
strips

8 ounces cooked chicken
or turkey breast, cut
into bite-size pieces

- For pesto, place basil, sweet pepper, mayonnaise,
Parmesan cheese, lemon juice, salt, ground red pepper,
and ground black pepper in a blender container or food
processor bowl. Cover and blend or process until nearly
smooth. Set pesto aside.

- Cook the pasta according to the directions on page 9,
adding carrots and onion during the last 4 minutes of
cooking time and zucchini and/or yellow squash during
the last 2 minutes. Drain pasta mixture; return to pan.

- Stir the pesto into pasta mixture; add chicken or turkey.
Toss well to combine. Cook over very low heat about 2
minutes or until heated through, tossing occasionally.
Makes 4 servings.

Flavor-Packed Parmesan

Bring out the best in pasta dishes by sprinkling them with
golden Parmesan cheese. This long-time pasta partner has a
sharp, pleasantly salty taste. The longer the cheese is aged, the
more robust its flavor. You can buy both domestic and imported
versions in chunks as well as in shredded and grated forms. (If
you can't find fresh Parmesan cheese at your store—or just
want a change of taste—try Romano cheese. This hard, grating
cheese has a slightly stronger flavor and aroma than Parmesan.)

Parmesan purists insist that the only way to enjoy the cheese is
to freshly grate or shred it over each serving of pasta. To serve
the cheese this way, look for a small cheese grater at a cookware
shop. Use a light hand when you're grating or shredding on the
Parmesan, however, because too much cheese will overwhelm
the other flavors in the dish.

Red Pepper Pasta Primavera

Manicotti with Chive Cream Sauce

Per serving:
291 cal. (36% from fat), 22 g pro., 24 g carbo., 12 g fat,
48 mg cholesterol, 2 g dietary fiber, 222 mg sodium.

Preparation time:
30 minutes

Baking time:
25 minutes

Tender manicotti are stuffed with a chicken and broccoli filling, then baked in a smooth cheese sauce.

1 10-ounce package frozen chopped broccoli

12 packaged dried manicotti shells

1 8-ounce container soft-style cream cheese with chives and onion

⅔ cup milk

¼ cup grated Romano or Parmesan cheese

½ of a 7-ounce jar roasted red sweet peppers

2 cups chopped cooked chicken

¼ teaspoon ground black pepper

- Place broccoli in a colander, such as the Tupperware® Double Colander. Thaw broccoli by running under cold water; drain well. Cook, rinse, and drain the pasta according to the directions on page 9.

- Meanwhile, for sauce, stir cream cheese in a small heavy saucepan over medium-low heat until melted. Slowly add milk, stirring until smooth. Stir in Romano or Parmesan cheese.

- For filling, drain and slice roasted peppers. Stir together *¾ cup* of the sauce, the broccoli, roasted peppers, chicken, and ground black pepper in a mixing bowl. To fill manicotti shells, spoon about *⅓ cup* of the filling into *each* cooked shell.

- Place filled shells in a 3-quart rectangular baking dish. Pour remaining sauce over shells. Sprinkle with paprika, if desired. Cover and bake in a 350° oven for 25 to 30 minutes or until heated through. Makes 6 servings.

Turkey Tetrazzini

Per serving:
410 cal. (26% from fat), 25 g pro., 50 g carbo., 12 g fat,
54 mg cholesterol, 1 g dietary fiber, 403 mg sodium.

Preparation time:
25 minutes

Baking time:
10 minutes

Remember this tantalizing recipe the next time you have cooked turkey or chicken on hand.

6 ounces packaged dried spaghetti

1½ cups sliced fresh mushrooms

½ cup chopped green or red sweet pepper

¼ cup all-purpose flour

1 12-ounce can evaporated milk

1 teaspoon instant chicken bouillon granules

1 cup chopped cooked turkey or chicken

2 tablespoons dry sherry or water

Nonstick spray coating

2 tablespoons grated Parmesan cheese

2 tablespoons sliced almonds

- Cook, rinse, and drain the pasta according to the directions on page 9.

- Meanwhile, cook mushrooms and sweet pepper in a small amount of boiling water in a large covered saucepan about 3 minutes or until vegetables are tender. Drain well.

- Stir together flour and ½ cup *cold water* in a small bowl. Stir into the vegetable mixture in saucepan. Stir in milk, bouillon granules, and ⅛ teaspoon *ground black pepper.* Cook and stir until thickened and bubbly. Stir in the pasta, turkey or chicken, and dry sherry or water.

- Spray a 2-quart square baking dish with nonstick spray coating. Pour the pasta mixture into the dish. Sprinkle with Parmesan cheese and almonds. Bake, uncovered, in a 400° oven about 10 minutes or until heated through. Makes 4 servings.

Lasagna Roll-Ups

Per serving:
524 cal. (30% from fat), 26 g pro., 67 g carbo., 18 g fat,
50 mg cholesterol, 6 g dietary fiber, 860 mg sodium.

Preparation time:
35 minutes

Baking time:
35 minutes

Work-saving no-boil noodles and bottled spaghetti sauce streamline the preparation of these turkey-filled rolls.

8   packaged dried no-boil or regular lasagna noodles

1   small eggplant, peeled

12   ounces ground raw turkey

½   cup sliced celery

2½   cups bottled spaghetti sauce

½   teaspoon dried Italian seasoning, crushed

¼   teaspoon garlic powder

- Soak the no-boil lasagna noodles in warm water for 10 minutes. Drain well. (*Or*, cook, rinse, and drain the regular lasagna noodles according to the directions on page 9.)

- Cut twelve ¼-inch-thick slices crosswise from the bottom of the eggplant; halve each slice, forming semicircles. Set aside. Chop the remaining eggplant (you should have about 1 cup).

- Cook the chopped eggplant, the turkey, and celery in a large skillet about 5 minutes or until the turkey no longer is pink and the eggplant is tender. Drain mixture well. Stir in *1 cup* of the spaghetti sauce, the Italian seasoning, and garlic powder.

- Spread *½ cup* of the remaining spaghetti sauce in the bottom of a 2-quart square baking dish. Spread about *⅓ cup* turkey mixture on *each* lasagna noodle. Roll up from one end. Place rolls, seam side down, in the dish. Place halved eggplant slices upright around edge of the dish, rounded edge up, overlapping slightly. Spoon the remaining spaghetti sauce over rolls.

- Cover and bake in a 375° oven about 35 minutes or until filling is heated through and pasta is tender. Garnish with parsley, oregano, and chive sprigs, if desired. Makes 4 servings.

Use Your Microwave

Follow these steps for a speedy microwave version of Lasagna Roll-Ups you can make in about half the time.

Soak or cook the lasagna noodles and slice and chop the eggplant as directed in the recipe above. Crumble the ground turkey into a 1½-quart microwave-safe casserole. Add the chopped eggplant and the celery. Micro-cook, covered, on 100% power (high) for 5 to 7 minutes or until the turkey no longer is pink and the eggplant is tender; stir once. Drain well. Stir in *1 cup* of the spaghetti sauce.

Assemble the lasagna rolls as directed in the recipe above, using a microwave-safe 2-quart square baking dish. Cover with waxed paper. Cook on high for 10 to 12 minutes or until heated through and pasta is tender, giving the dish a half-turn once.

Herbed Almond and Chicken Linguine
made with three-pepper linguine

Herbed Almond and Chicken Linguine

Per serving:
451 cal. (29% from fat), 29 g pro., 50 g carbo., 14 g fat,
66 mg cholesterol, 3 g dietary fiber, 247 mg sodium.

**Preparation time:
25 minutes**

Three-pepper linguine
adds a hint of hotness to
this Oriental stir-fry. To
make your own pepper-
flavored pasta, see the
recipe on page 8.

8	ounces packaged dried linguine
¾	cup chicken broth
2	tablespoons dry sherry or water
2	teaspoons cornstarch
½	teaspoon dried savory, crushed
¼	teaspoon dried thyme, crushed
2	tablespoons cooking oil
1	clove garlic, minced
2	medium carrots, thinly bias-sliced
¼	cup green onions bias-sliced into 1-inch pieces
¼	cup sliced almonds
12	ounces skinless, boneless chicken breast halves, cut into bite-size pieces
	Chive stems (optional)
	Thyme sprigs (optional)

- Cook pasta according to directions on page 9. Drain the pasta; cover to keep warm.

- Meanwhile, for sauce, stir together chicken broth, sherry or water, cornstarch, savory, and thyme in a small bowl. Set aside.

- Pour cooking oil into a wok or large skillet. (Add more oil as necessary during cooking.) Heat over medium-high heat. Add garlic; stir-fry for 15 seconds. Add carrots; stir-fry for 3 minutes. Add green onions and almonds; stir-fry about 2 minutes more or until onion is crisp-tender. Remove mixture from wok.

- Add chicken to the wok or skillet. Stir-fry for 2 to 3 minutes or until chicken is tender and no longer pink. Drain off fat. Push chicken from center of the wok or skillet. Stir sauce; add to center of the wok or skillet. Cook and stir until thickened and bubbly. Return vegetable mixture to the wok or skillet; stir chicken and vegetables together to coat with sauce. Cook and stir for 1 minute more.

- To serve, toss the chicken mixture with the pasta. Garnish with chive stems and thyme sprigs, if desired. Makes 4 servings.

Bias-Slicing Vegetables

Make stir-fries and other dishes more attractive by bias-slicing the vegetables. These elongated slices not only make the vegetables more interesting looking, they also cook more quickly because they have more exposed surface area than straight-cut slices. To bias-slice, hold a sharp knife or cleaver at a 45-degree angle and cut the food into evenly thick slices.

Ham and Blue Cheese Pasta Salad

Per serving:
501 cal. (56% from fat), 16 g pro., 40 g carbo., 32 g fat,
21 mg cholesterol, 2 g dietary fiber, 464 mg sodium.

**Preparation time:
40 minutes**

Rigatoni and crunchy pecans team with tangy blue cheese for a full-flavored salad. If you have corkscrew macaroni on hand, you can substitute it for the rigatoni.

4   ounces fully cooked ham

1   cup broken pecans, toasted

½   to ¾ cup crumbled blue cheese (2 to 3 ounces)

⅓   cup snipped parsley

¼   cup olive or salad oil

1   teaspoon dried rosemary, crushed

1   clove garlic, minced

½   teaspoon coarsely ground pepper

8   ounces packaged dried rigatoni

- Cut ham into bite-size strips. Combine ham, pecans, blue cheese, parsley, oil, rosemary, garlic, and pepper in a very large mixing bowl. Cover and let stand at room temperature for 30 minutes.

- Meanwhile, cook, rinse, and drain the pasta according to the directions on page 9. Toss pasta with ham mixture.

- To serve, line serving platter with salad greens, if desired. Spoon the pasta mixture over the salad greens. Makes 5 servings.

Fettuccine with Chicken

Per serving:
480 cal. (32% from fat), 37 g pro., 42 g carbo., 17 g fat,
86 mg cholesterol, 2 g dietary fiber, 649 mg sodium.

**Preparation time:
30 minutes**

Nutmeg subtly accents the sherry sauce to make this dish scrumptious.

6   ounces packaged dried fettuccine

1½   cups sliced fresh mushrooms

¼   cup sliced green onions

2   tablespoons margarine or butter

2   tablespoons all-purpose flour

¼   teaspoon salt

¼   teaspoon ground nutmeg

¼   teaspoon pepper

1½   cups milk

½   cup grated Parmesan cheese

2   tablespoons dry sherry or chicken broth

2   cups cubed cooked chicken

½   cup sliced pitted ripe olives

- Cook, rinse, and drain the pasta according to the directions on page 9.

- Meanwhile, for sauce, cook mushrooms and green onions in margarine or butter in a 12-inch skillet about 5 minutes or until vegetables are tender. Stir in flour, salt, nutmeg, and pepper. Add milk all at once. Cook and stir until thickened and bubbly. Cook and stir for 1 minute more. Add *half* of the Parmesan cheese and the sherry or chicken broth; heat until cheese is melted.

- Add pasta, chicken, and ripe olives to skillet. Stir to coat with sauce. Heat through.

- To serve, sprinkle with the remaining Parmesan cheese. Garnish with snipped chives and serve with lemon wedges, if desired. Makes 4 servings.

Ham and Blue Cheese Pasta Salad

Fettuccine with Herbed Shrimp

Per serving:
391 cal. (18% from fat), 26 g pro., 52 g carbo., 8 g fat,
142 mg cholesterol, 3 g dietary fiber, 948 mg sodium.

**Preparation time:
30 minutes**

A delicious white wine and mushroom sauce lightly coats the shrimp and pasta in this elegant entrée.

8 ounces packaged dried fettuccine

12 ounces fresh peeled and deveined shrimp*

2 medium tomatoes

2 cups sliced fresh mushrooms

1 cup chopped onion

2 cloves garlic, minced

1 tablespoon cooking oil

¼ cup dry white wine or water

1 tablespoon instant chicken bouillon granules

1 tablespoon fresh snipped basil or 1 teaspoon dried basil, crushed

1½ teaspoons fresh snipped oregano or ½ teaspoon dried oregano, crushed

1 teaspoon cornstarch

⅛ teaspoon pepper

¼ cup grated Parmesan cheese

¼ cup snipped parsley

- Cook the pasta according to the directions on page 9. Drain the pasta; cover to keep warm.

- Meanwhile, cut the shrimp in half lengthwise; set aside. Peel, seed, and chop tomatoes; set aside. Cook mushrooms, onion, and garlic in hot oil in a large saucepan until onion is tender but not brown. Drain fat.

- Stir together wine or water, bouillon granules, basil, oregano, cornstarch, and pepper. Add to saucepan. Cook and stir until thickened and bubbly.

- Stir shrimp into saucepan. Cover and simmer about 2 minutes or until shrimp turn pink. Stir in tomatoes; heat through.

- Serve the shrimp mixture over pasta. Sprinkle with grated Parmesan cheese and snipped parsley. Toss to mix. Makes 4 servings.

*If substituting shrimp in the shell, you'll need 18 ounces to give 12 ounces after peeling and deveining. (See tip, below.)

Shrimp Savvy

With a little practice you can become a master at peeling and deveining shrimp quickly.

Starting at the head end of the shrimp, use your fingers to open the shell lengthwise down the underside of the body. Peel back the shell, gently pulling on the tail portion of the shell to remove it.

To devein shrimp, use a sharp knife to make a shallow slit along the back from the head end to the tail. Rinse the slit under cold running water to remove the vein, using the tip of the knife, if necessary, to loosen the vein.

Creamy Salmon and Shells

Per serving:
301 cal. (23% from fat), 26 g pro., 29 g carbo., 8 g fat,
42 mg cholesterol, 0 g dietary fiber, 356 mg sodium.

Preparation time:
30 minutes

This sophisticated pasta dish can be assembled quickly for dinner guests. Serve it with steamed asparagus and hard rolls.

12	ounces fresh or frozen salmon fillets
1½	cups dry white wine or water
4	ounces packaged dried small shells (1 cup)
½	cup plain yogurt
2	tablespoons all-purpose flour
¾	cup chicken broth
¼	cup milk
1	teaspoon Dijon-style mustard
	Dash ground red pepper
½	cup thinly sliced celery
2	tablespoons grated Parmesan cheese

- Measure thickness of fish fillets. Bring wine or water to boiling in a large skillet. Add fish. Return to boiling; reduce heat. Cover and simmer until fish just flakes when tested with a fork (allow 4 to 6 minutes per ½-inch thickness of fish for fresh fish or 6 to 9 minutes per ½-inch thickness for frozen fish). Drain fish, discarding liquid. Cut fish into bite-size pieces.

- Meanwhile, cook pasta according to directions on page 9. Drain pasta; cover to keep warm.

- Stir together yogurt and flour in a medium bowl. Stir in chicken broth, milk, mustard, and red pepper. Transfer mixture to skillet. Add celery. Cook and stir until thickened and bubbly. Cook and stir 1 minute more. (Mixture may appear curdled until fully cooked.) Add pasta, tossing to coat. Gently fold in fish pieces and Parmesan cheese. Heat mixture through. Season to taste with *salt* and *pepper*.

- To serve, sprinkle with snipped chives and paprika, if desired. Makes 4 servings.

Speedy Salmon Rigatoni

Per serving:
457 cal. (32% from fat), 24 g pro., 55 g carbo., 16 g fat,
26 mg cholesterol, 2 g dietary fiber, 621 mg sodium.

Preparation time:
25 minutes

A dill-flavored cheese sauce accents this tantalizing trio of salmon, spinach, and rigatoni.

½	of a 10-ounce package frozen chopped spinach
8	ounces packaged dried rigatoni
1	cup sliced fresh mushrooms
½	cup chopped onion
2	tablespoons margarine or butter
2	tablespoons all-purpose flour
¼	teaspoon dried dillweed
1¼	cups milk
¾	cup shredded process American cheese
1	6½-ounce can skinless, boneless salmon
2	tablespoons snipped parsley

- Place chopped spinach in a colander, such as the Tupperware® Double Colander. Thaw spinach by running under cold water; drain well. Cook pasta according to the directions on page 9, adding the spinach during the last 2 minutes of cooking time. Drain the pasta mixture; cover to keep warm.

- Meanwhile, cook mushrooms and onion in margarine or butter in a medium saucepan until vegetables are tender. Stir in flour and dillweed. Add milk all at once. Cook and stir until thickened and bubbly. Cook and stir for 1 minute more. Add American cheese, stirring just until melted.

- Drain the salmon. Stir the salmon and parsley into the sauce. Heat through.

- To serve, toss salmon mixture and pasta mixture gently until pasta is coated. Makes 4 servings.

Shrimp and Fusilli

Linguine with Clams and Dried Tomatoes

Per serving:
393 cal. (23% from fat), 21 g pro., 49 g carbo., 10 g fat,
45 mg cholesterol, 2 g dietary fiber, 178 mg sodium.

Preparation time: 25 minutes

Dried tomatoes impart a robust, slightly tangy flavor to this classic pasta dish. Look for them in the produce or gourmet section of the supermarket.

8	ounces packaged dried linguine or fettuccine
2	6½-ounce cans chopped or minced clams
½	cup chopped onion
2	cloves garlic, minced
¼	teaspoon crushed red pepper
2	tablespoons cooking oil
½	cup dry white wine or chicken broth
⅓	cup oil-packed dried tomatoes
2	tablespoons snipped parsley

- Cook the pasta according to the directions on page 9. Drain the pasta; cover to keep warm.

- Meanwhile, drain clams, reserving liquid. Cook onion, garlic, and red pepper in hot oil in a medium saucepan until onion is tender. Drain off fat. Stir reserved clam liquid and wine or chicken broth into saucepan.

- Bring to boiling; reduce heat. Boil gently about 10 minutes or until reduced to 1 cup. Drain dried tomatoes and cut into strips. Stir clams, dried tomatoes, and snipped parsley into saucepan; heat through.

- Serve the clam mixture over pasta. Garnish with parsley sprigs, if desired. Makes 4 servings.

Shrimp and Fusilli

Per serving:
419 cal. (20% from fat), 27 g pro., 56 g carbo., 9 g fat,
143 mg cholesterol, 3 g dietary fiber, 485 mg sodium.

Preparation time: 30 minutes

Fresh shrimp and a lemon yogurt sauce make this colorful pasta dish refreshingly pleasing to the palate.

12	ounces fresh peeled and deveined shrimp*
8	ounces packaged dried fusilli or linguine
2	cups broccoli flowerets
2	medium onions
2	cloves garlic, minced
2	tablespoons margarine or butter
1	tablespoon all-purpose flour
1	teaspoon instant chicken bouillon granules
⅛	teaspoon pepper
1	cup milk
½	cup plain yogurt
2	tablespoons dry sherry or water
¾	teaspoon finely shredded lemon peel
	Cracked black pepper

- Cut shrimp in half lengthwise. Cook shrimp in boiling water for 1 to 3 minutes or until shrimp turn pink, stirring occasionally. Drain shrimp; cover to keep warm.

- Meanwhile, cook the pasta according to the directions on page 9, adding broccoli during the last 8 minutes of cooking time. Drain pasta mixture; cover to keep warm.

- Cut onions into thin wedges. Cook onions and garlic in margarine or butter in a medium saucepan until the onions are tender but not brown.

- Stir flour, chicken bouillon granules, and ⅛ teaspoon pepper into saucepan. Add milk all at once. Cook and stir over medium heat until thickened and bubbly. Cook and stir for 1 minute more. Stir in yogurt, sherry or water, and lemon peel. Heat until the mixture is just warm (do not boil).

- Stir shrimp into saucepan. Gently toss shrimp mixture with pasta mixture until pasta is coated. Sprinkle with cracked pepper. Garnish with lemon slices and whole cooked shrimp with tails, if desired. Makes 4 servings.

*If substituting shrimp in the shell, you'll need 18 ounces to give 12 ounces after peeling and deveining. (See tip, page 52.)

Macaroni and Lots of Cheese

Per serving:
620 cal. (48% from fat), 28 g pro., 54 g carbo., 33 g fat,
84 mg cholesterol, 0 g dietary fiber, 592 mg sodium.

Preparation time:
25 minutes

Baking time:
20 minutes

Three different cheeses make this home-style casserole creamy and wonderfully tangy.

8   ounces packaged dried corkscrew macaroni

¼   cup finely chopped green onions

2   tablespoons margarine or butter

2   tablespoons all-purpose flour

⅛   teaspoon pepper

2   cups milk

1½ cups shredded sharp cheddar cheese (6 ounces)

1   3-ounce package cream cheese, cubed and softened

⅓   cup grated Parmesan cheese

1   medium tomato, cut into wedges (optional)

     Sliced green onions (optional)

• Cook, rinse, and drain the pasta according to the directions on page 9.

• Meanwhile, cook chopped green onions in margarine or butter in a large saucepan until onions are tender. Stir in flour and pepper. Add the milk all at once. Cook and stir over medium heat until thickened and bubbly. Gradually add the cheddar cheese and cream cheese, stirring until melted. Gently stir the pasta into the cheese mixture. Transfer to a greased 1½-quart casserole. Sprinkle with Parmesan cheese.

• Bake, uncovered, in a 350° oven for 20 to 25 minutes or until heated through. Garnish with tomato wedges and sliced green onions, if desired. Makes 4 servings.

Microwave It!

No time—or just too hot in the kitchen—to bake? Then try this microwave version of Macaroni and Lots of Cheese.

Cook, rinse, and drain the pasta according to the directions on page 9. Micro-cook margarine or butter and chopped green onions, covered, in the Tupperware® 1¾-quart TupperWave® casserole on 100% power (high) for 1½ to 2½ minutes or until tender. Stir in flour and pepper. Add milk all at once. Stir to combine ingredients.

Cook, uncovered, on high for 6 to 8 minutes or until thickened and bubbly, stirring after every minute until the mixture starts to thicken, then stirring every 30 seconds. Gradually add the cheddar cheese and cream cheese, stirring until nearly melted. Gently stir the pasta into the cheese mixture.

Cook, uncovered, on high for 3 minutes; stir. Sprinkle with Parmesan cheese. Cook, uncovered, on high for 2 to 4 minutes more or until heated through. Serve as directed in recipe above.

Cheese-Stuffed Manicotti

Per serving:
403 cal. (33% from fat), 28 g pro., 40 g carbo., 15 g fat,
50 mg cholesterol, 4 g dietary fiber, 962 mg sodium.

Preparation time:
45 minutes

Baking time:
35 minutes

If you want to cut the prep time of this enticing dish, use your favorite bottled spaghetti sauce instead of starting from scratch.

8   packaged dried manicotti shells

2   slightly beaten egg whites

1¾ cups ricotta cheese, drained

1   cup shredded mozzarella cheese (4 ounces)

2   tablespoons snipped parsley

1   tablespoon grated Parmesan cheese

½   teaspoon dried Italian seasoning, crushed

¼   teaspoon salt

¼   teaspoon pepper

Savory Tomato Sauce (see tip, below) or 3 cups bottled meatless spaghetti sauce

- Cook, rinse, and drain the pasta according to the directions on page 9.

- For filling, stir together egg whites, ricotta cheese, mozzarella cheese, snipped parsley, Parmesan cheese, Italian seasoning, salt, and pepper in a mixing bowl.

- To fill manicotti shells, spoon about ⅓ cup of the filling into *each* cooked shell. Arrange filled shells in a 2-quart rectangular baking dish. Pour the sauce over shells.

- Cover and bake in a 350° oven for 35 to 40 minutes or until heated through.

- To serve, garnish manicotti with parsley sprigs, if desired. Makes 4 servings.

Note: Pictured on pages 24–25.

Savory Tomato Sauce

Use this robust sauce in the recipe above or serve it over your favorite pasta as a flavorful side dish.

Stir together 1 cup chopped *onion*, ½ cup coarsely chopped *green pepper*, ½ cup shredded *carrot*, ½ cup sliced *celery*, ½ cup *water*, and 2 cloves *garlic*, minced, in a medium saucepan. Bring to boiling; reduce heat. Cover and simmer about 5 minutes or until vegetables are tender. *Do not drain.*

Cut up one 14½-ounce can *tomatoes*. Stir *undrained* tomatoes, ⅓ cup *tomato paste*, 1 teaspoon *Italian seasoning* (crushed), ½ teaspoon *sugar*, ¼ teaspoon *salt*, and ⅛ teaspoon *pepper* into saucepan. Bring to boiling; reduce heat. Cover and simmer for 15 minutes, stirring often. Makes about 3 cups.

Per serving of sauce: 71 cal. (7% from fat), 3 g pro., 16 g carbo., 1 g fat,
0 mg cholesterol, 4 g dietary fiber, 491 mg sodium.

Light and
Luscious Entrées

Pasta dishes are perfect for great-tasting low-calorie dining—as the recipes in this section attest. All are under 350 calories per serving, and no more than 30 percent of their calories come from fat. From sumptuous soups and stews to irresistible lasagna, you'll find a hearty helping of deliciously light recipes here.

Spaghetti alla Carbonara
(See recipe, page 74.)

Meatball Soup

Per serving:
307 cal. (22% from fat), 26 g pro., 36 g carbo.. 8 g fat,
85 mg cholesterol, 5 g dietary fiber, 1,142 mg sodium.

**Preparation time:
35 minutes**

Serve warm corn muffins
or Italian breadsticks with
this hearty soup filled
with Parmesan-seasoned
meatballs.

Parmesan Meatballs
(see recipe, below
right)

1 15-ounce can garbanzo
   beans

1 14½-ounce can beef
   broth

1 14½-ounce can Italian-
   style stewed tomatoes

1 cup sliced fresh
   mushrooms or one
   4½-ounce jar sliced
   mushrooms, drained

1 teaspoon dried Italian
   seasoning, crushed

1 ounce packaged dried
   tiny bows (½ cup)

3 cups torn fresh spinach

- Prepare Parmesan Meatballs. Cook meatballs in a large
  skillet over medium heat about 8 minutes or until no
  pink remains, turning occasionally to brown evenly.
  Drain off fat. Set meatballs aside.

- Meanwhile, rinse and drain garbanzo beans. Stir
  together beans, beef broth, *undrained* tomatoes,
  mushrooms, and Italian seasoning in a large saucepan.
  Stir in 1½ cups *water*. Bring to boiling. Add *uncooked*
  pasta. Return to boiling; reduce heat. Cover and simmer
  for 10 to 12 minutes or until pasta is tender, adding the
  meatballs during the last 5 minutes of the cooking time.
  Stir in spinach. Cook for 1 to 2 minutes more or just
  until spinach is wilted. Makes 4 servings.

Parmesan Meatballs: Combine 1 beaten *egg*, ½ cup
soft bread crumbs, 2 tablespoons grated *Parmesan
cheese,* 1 tablespoon snipped *parsley,* 1 tablespoon finely
chopped *onion,* ¼ teaspoon *garlic salt,* and ⅛ teaspoon
pepper in a mixing bowl. Add 8 ounces 90% lean *ground
beef;* mix well. Shape meat mixture into 36 meatballs.

Easy Chili Skillet

Per serving:
279 cal. (17% from fat), 24 g pro., 36 g carbo., 5 g fat,
35 mg cholesterol, 9 g dietary fiber, 911 mg sodium.

**Preparation time:
35 minutes**

Adjust the hotness to suit
your family, choosing mild
or hot chili powder. Keep
in mind, too, that a dollop
of plain yogurt or a glass
of milk will tame spicy
foods for those who like
their dishes a bit tamer
than others.

8 ounces 90% lean
   ground beef

½ cup chopped onion

1 15½-ounce can red
   kidney beans, rinsed
   and drained

1 8-ounce can tomato
   sauce

½ of a 14½-ounce can
   tomatoes, cut up

2 ounces packaged dried
   elbow macaroni (½ cup)

½ cup chopped green
   pepper

¼ cup water

1 tablespoon chili powder

½ teaspoon garlic salt

¼ cup shredded lower-fat
   Monterey Jack or
   cheddar cheese (1 ounce)

- Cook meat and onion in a large skillet until meat is
  brown. Drain off fat. Stir in kidney beans, tomato sauce,
  undrained tomatoes, *uncooked* pasta, green pepper,
  water, chili powder, and garlic salt. Bring to boiling;
  reduce heat. Cover; simmer for 20 minutes, stirring often.

- To serve, remove skillet from heat. Sprinkle meat
  mixture with Monterey Jack or cheddar cheese. Cover
  and let stand about 2 minutes or until the cheese melts.
  Makes 4 servings.

Family-Favorite Lasagna

Per serving:
290 cal. (25% from fat), 24 g pro., 32 g carbo., 8 g fat,
36 mg cholesterol, 3 g dietary fiber, 722 mg sodium.

Preparation time:
30 minutes

Baking time:
25 minutes

Standing time:
10 minutes

Want to serve lasagna, but your schedule for the day is jam-packed? Here's an easy solution. Assemble the lasagna the night before. Cover and store it in the refrigerator up to 24 hours. Then at meal time, bake the casserole for 40 to 45 minutes.

4   ounces 90% lean ground beef

½   cup chopped onion

½   cup finely chopped carrot

2   cloves garlic, minced

1   8-ounce can tomato sauce

⅓   cup tomato paste

¼   cup water

1   teaspoon dried basil, crushed

½   teaspoon dried oregano, crushed

½   teaspoon fennel seed, crushed

4   packaged dried lasagna noodles

1   egg white

1   cup nonfat or part-skim ricotta cheese, drained

    Nonstick spray coating

½   cup shredded part-skim mozzarella cheese (2 ounces)

2   tablespoons grated Parmesan cheese

- For sauce, cook the meat, onion, carrot, and garlic in a medium saucepan until meat is brown and vegetables are tender. Drain off fat. Stir in tomato sauce, tomato paste, water, basil, oregano, fennel seed, and ¼ teaspoon *pepper*. Bring to boiling; reduce heat. Cover and simmer for 10 minutes, stirring occasionally.

- Meanwhile, cook, rinse, and drain the pasta according to the directions on page 9.

- For ricotta mixture, slightly beat the egg white in a small mixing bowl; stir in the ricotta cheese.

- Spray a 2-quart square baking dish with nonstick spray coating. Place *2* of the cooked noodles in the dish. (If necessary, cut noodles to fit dish.) Spread with *half* of the ricotta mixture. Top with *half* of the sauce and *half* of the mozzarella cheese. Repeat layers. Sprinkle with Parmesan cheese.

- Bake, uncovered, in a 375° oven for 25 to 30 minutes or until heated through. Let stand for 10 minutes before serving. Sprinkle lasagna with snipped parsley, if desired. Makes 4 servings.

Ricotta Cheese Choices

The creamy richness in this lasagna comes from ricotta cheese, of which three types are commonly available. To keep calories and fat under control, choose part-skim ricotta (170 calories and 10 grams of fat in a ½ cup) or nonfat ricotta (90 calories and 0 grams of fat in a ½ cup). When compared with the same amount of regular whole-milk ricotta (214 calories and 16 grams of fat), the difference is obvious. If you prefer the flavor of cottage cheese, you can use it in place of the ricotta cheese. With only 109 calories and 5 grams of fat for a ½ cup of cream-style cottage cheese, you can make this substitution confident that the dish is still healthful and delicious.

Pasta with Chicken and Shrimp

Pasta with Chicken and Shrimp

Per serving:
340 cal. (10% from fat), 27 g pro., 49 g carbo., 4 g fat,
90 mg cholesterol, 2 g dietary fiber, 720 mg sodium.

Preparation time:
30 minutes

Flavored with a hint of ginger this stir-fry is great for entertaining. Complete the menu with steamed broccoli or asparagus spears, a mixed greens salad, and whole-wheat rolls.

½ cup chicken broth

2 tablespoons soy sauce

2 teaspoons cornstarch

½ teaspoon ground ginger

8 ounces skinless, boneless chicken breast halves or turkey breast tenderloin steak

8 ounces packaged dried linguine

Nonstick spray coating

½ cup green onions cut into ½-inch pieces

2 cloves garlic, minced

1 to 2 teaspoons cooking oil (if needed)

1 yellow summer squash, sliced (1¼ cups)

1 small red or green sweet pepper, cut into thin strips

4 ounces fresh peeled and deveined medium shrimp*

- Combine chicken broth, soy sauce, cornstarch, and ginger in a small mixing bowl; set aside. Cut chicken or turkey into ¾-inch pieces; set aside.

- Cook the pasta according to the directions on page 9. Drain the pasta; cover to keep warm.

- Meanwhile, spray a cold wok or large skillet with nonstick spray coating. Preheat wok or skillet over medium heat. Add green onions and garlic; stir-fry for 1 minute. (Add oil if necessary during cooking.) Remove from wok. Add squash to wok; stir-fry for 1½ minutes. Add red or green pepper; stir-fry about 1½ minutes more or until vegetables are crisp-tender. Remove from wok.

- Add chicken or turkey and shrimp to wok or skillet. Stir-fry for 3 to 4 minutes or until chicken is tender and no longer pink and shrimp turn pink. Push chicken and shrimp from the center of the wok.

- Stir broth mixture; add to center of the wok. Cook and stir until thickened and bubbly. Return all of the cooked vegetables to wok; stir all ingredients together to coat with sauce. Cook and stir about 1 minute more or until heated through.

- Serve the chicken mixture over pasta. Garnish with summer squash slices, a cherry tomato cut into a tulip, and a ripe olive, if desired. Makes 4 servings.

*If substituting shrimp in the shell, you'll need 6 ounces to give 4 ounces after peeling and deveining. (See tip, page 52.)

Become a Sodium Sleuth

If you want to track the sodium in your diet, look for the many lower-sodium food products now available. In the canned vegetable aisle of your supermarket, you'll find sodium-reduced versions of tomato paste, tomato sauce, tomatoes, kidney beans, and other vegetables. Elsewhere in the store, you'll find lower-sodium soy sauce, chicken broth, beef and chicken bouillon, canned soup, and cheese. Substitute these products for their regular counterparts in recipes and lower the sodium in dishes substantially.

Chicken Rigatoni with Tomato Sauce

Per serving:
308 cal. (24% from fat), 22 g pro., 37 g carbo., 8 g fat,
47 mg cholesterol, 3 g dietary fiber, 380 mg sodium.

**Preparation time:
40 minutes**

Kids will love the Italian flavor of this dish, and parents will love how easy and convenient it is to make.

½ cup chopped onion

1 clove garlic, minced

1 tablespoon cooking oil

1 16-ounce can tomatoes, cut up

1 7½-ounce can tomatoes, cut up

5 ounces packaged dried rigatoni (about 2 cups)

1¼ cups water

1 2½-ounce jar sliced mushrooms, drained

1 teaspoon dried Italian seasoning, crushed

1½ cups chopped cooked chicken or turkey

- Cook onion and garlic in hot oil in a large saucepan until onion is tender but not brown.

- Stir in *undrained* tomatoes, *uncooked* pasta, water, mushrooms, and Italian seasoning. Bring to boiling; reduce heat. Cover and simmer about 20 minutes or until pasta is just tender, stirring occasionally.

- Stir in chicken or turkey; heat through. Garnish with basil leaves, if desired. Makes 4 servings.

Chicken-Vegetable Noodle Soup

Per serving:
229 cal. (22% from fat), 22 g pro., 24 g carbo., 6 g fat,
73 mg cholesterol, 3 g dietary fiber, 979 mg sodium.

**Preparation time:
45 minutes**

**Cooking time:
1 hour 15 minutes**

To save calories—and cut last-minute preparation time—do the first two steps of this recipe the day before, then refrigerate the broth and chopped chicken separately. That will make it easier to remove the fat from the broth—and on meal day you can have dinner on the table in less than 30 minutes.

2 pounds meaty chicken pieces, skinned*

2 tablespoons instant chicken bouillon granules

1 teaspoon dried marjoram or basil, crushed

½ teaspoon ground black pepper

1 clove garlic, halved

1 10-ounce package frozen succotash

3 ounces packaged dried medium or wide noodles (about 1½ cups)

1 cup chopped onion

½ cup chopped green or red sweet pepper

¼ cup snipped parsley

- Combine chicken, bouillon granules, marjoram or basil, ground black pepper, garlic, and 8 cups *water* in a Dutch oven. Bring to boiling; reduce heat. Cover and simmer about 1 hour or until the chicken is tender and no longer pink.

- Remove the chicken from the broth mixture; cool until easy to handle. Remove meat from bones. Cut meat into bite-size pieces; set aside. Discard bones. Strain broth.

- Skim fat from broth. Return broth to pan. Add succotash, *uncooked* pasta, onion, and sweet pepper to the broth. Return to boiling; reduce heat. Simmer, uncovered, about 10 minutes or until the pasta is just tender. Stir in parsley and cooked chicken. Heat through. Makes 6 servings.

*Use chicken breasts, thighs, and/or drumsticks.

Mandarin Chicken with Noodles

Per serving:
298 cal. (27% from fat), 31 g pro., 24 g carbo., 9 g fat,
72 mg cholesterol, 3 g dietary fiber, 402 mg sodium.

**Preparation time:
30 minutes**

Sweet-and-sour sauce and mandarin oranges add just the right touch of the Orient to this stir-fry.

Nonstick spray coating

1   pound skinless, boneless chicken breast halves, cut into bite-size strips

1   3-ounce package Oriental noodles with chicken-flavor packet

1   small zucchini or yellow summer squash, halved lengthwise and bias sliced

2   stalks celery, thinly bias sliced

1   cup water

2   cloves garlic, minced

¼   cup bottled sweet-and-sour sauce

2   tablespoons coarsely chopped peanuts

1   11-ounce can mandarin orange sections, drained

● Spray a cold wok or large skillet with nonstick spray coating. Preheat wok over medium heat. Stir-fry chicken, half at a time, in wok about 3 minutes or until chicken is tender and no longer pink; remove from wok.

● Break up the Oriental noodles (set flavor packet aside). Add *uncooked* Oriental noodles, zucchini, celery, water, and garlic to wok. Bring to boiling; reduce heat. Cover; simmer for 3 to 5 minutes or until noodles and vegetables are tender.

● Stir in chicken, the flavor packet from noodles, sweet-and-sour sauce, and peanuts; heat through. Spoon into serving dish. Top with the mandarin orange sections. Makes 4 servings.

Poultry Pointers

To be sure the poultry you serve is at its peak in quality, flavor, and safety remember these tips.

Refrigerate poultry as soon as possible after purchasing and keep it in the coldest part of the refrigerator for a maximum of two days. For longer storage, freeze it in a Tupperware® freezer container for up to six months.

Avoid thawing poultry at room temperature. Thaw it in your refrigerator. (Or, check your microwave oven owner's manual for thawing directions.)

Wash your hands, utensils, and work surfaces with hot soapy water after handling raw poultry to prevent spreading bacteria to other foods.

Use one dish for raw poultry and another for the cooked.

Leave cooked poultry at room temperature for no more than two hours.

20-Minute
Hearty Soup

Per serving:
285 cal. (10% from fat), 26 g pro., 40 g carbo., 3 g fat,
34 mg cholesterol, 8 g dietary fiber, 1,449 mg sodium.

Preparation time:
20 minutes

Intrigue the children with
the wagon wheels floating
in this tasty fish soup.
Make it with cod, pike, or
orange roughy fillets or
choose chicken instead
of fish.

2   14½-ounce cans
    chicken broth

1   15-ounce can red
    kidney beans, rinsed
    and drained

1   cup loose-pack frozen
    mixed vegetables*

½   cup chopped onion

1½ ounces packaged dried
    wagon wheels (about
    ½ cup)

1   teaspoon dried basil or
    thyme, crushed

¼   teaspoon pepper

12 ounces fresh skinless
    fish fillets or skinless,
    boneless chicken breast
    halves

1   14½-ounce can Italian-
    style stewed tomatoes

- Stir together chicken broth, kidney beans, frozen
  vegetables, onion, *uncooked* pasta, basil or thyme, and
  pepper in a large saucepan. Bring to boiling; reduce
  heat. Cover and simmer for 10 minutes.

- Meanwhile, cut fish or chicken into 1-inch pieces. Stir
  fish or chicken and *undrained* stewed tomatoes into
  broth mixture. Return to boiling; reduce heat. Cover and
  simmer until fish just flakes when tested with a fork or
  chicken is tender and no longer pink, stirring once. (For
  fish, allow 2 to 3 minutes; for chicken, allow 4 to 5
  minutes.) Makes 4 servings.

*Mix two or three frozen vegetables to measure 1 cup or
use a frozen vegetable combination.

Ham, Bean,
and Pasta Soup

Per serving:
283 cal. (12% from fat), 20 g pro., 43 g carbo., 4 g fat,
19 mg cholesterol, 7 g dietary fiber, 1,093 mg sodium.

Preparation time:
20 minutes

Steaming bowls of this soup
are sure to chase away the
worst of winter's chills.

1   15-ounce can navy
    beans, rinsed and
    drained

2½ cups water

2   cups chicken broth

½   teaspoon dried
    marjoram or basil,
    crushed

¼   teaspoon pepper

4   ounces packaged dried
    elbow macaroni

1   cup cubed fully cooked
    ham or smoked turkey

½   cup chopped onion

½   cup sliced celery

- Mash about *half* of the navy beans with a fork or potato
  masher in a medium mixing bowl. Set whole and mashed
  navy beans aside.

- Combine water, chicken broth, marjoram or basil, and
  pepper in a large saucepan. Bring to boiling. Add the
  mashed and whole navy beans, *uncooked* pasta, ham or
  smoked turkey, onion, and celery to the broth mixture.

- Return to boiling; reduce heat. Simmer, uncovered, for
  10 to 15 minutes or until pasta is just tender, stirring
  occasionally. Makes 4 servings.

20-Minute Hearty Soup

Ham-and-Spinach Linguine

Per serving:
327 cal. (23% from fat), 31 g pro., 38 g carbo., 9 g fat,
48 mg cholesterol, 5 g dietary fiber, 1,701 mg sodium.

Preparation time:
30 minutes

Rinse the spinach and chop
or slice the ingredients
while the water is heating
so everything is ready to go
once cooking begins.

3	ounces packaged dried linguine
1	cup sliced fresh mushrooms
½	cup chopped onion
1	cup beef broth
½	cup skim milk
1	tablespoon cornstarch
½	teaspoon dried thyme or marjoram, crushed
8	ounces fully cooked ham, cut into thin strips
¼	cup snipped parsley
2	tablespoons Dijon-style mustard
6	ounces fresh spinach (6 cups)
1	tablespoon slivered almonds, toasted

- Cook the pasta according to the directions on page 9. Drain the pasta; cover to keep warm.

- Meanwhile, cook mushrooms and onion in beef broth in a large saucepan about 2 minutes or until the vegetables are just tender.

- Add skim milk and cornstarch to the Tupperware® Quick Shake® container. Apply seal and cap; shake well. Stir milk mixture and thyme into the saucepan. Cook and stir over medium-high heat until thickened and bubbly. Cook and stir for 1 minute more. Stir ham, parsley, and Dijon-style mustard into saucepan; heat through.

- Coarsely chop fresh spinach and arrange on a serving platter. Stir the pasta into ham mixture.

- Serve the ham-pasta mixture over spinach. Sprinkle with toasted almonds. Makes 3 servings.

Spinach at Its Peak

For fresh spinach at its most flavorful in recipes such as
Ham-and-Spinach Linguine, follow these hints.

Choose crisp, dark green, fresh-looking spinach; avoid bruised
or broken leaves.

Wash the leaves in cold water several times to remove any dirt
or sand, then pat them dry.

Store the cleaned spinach in a Tupperware® Easy-Crisp®
container for up to three days.

Cod Primavera
with Fettuccine

Per serving:
220 cal. (10% from fat), 22 g pro., 25 g carbo., 3 g fat,
40 mg cholesterol, 4 g dietary fiber, 335 mg sodium.

Preparation time:
30 minutes

For a '90s-style one-dish meal complete with pasta, crisp vegetables, and chunks of fish, it's hard to beat this primavera with its delicate wine sauce.

12	ounces fresh or frozen cod or other fish fillets
2	ounces packaged dried fettuccine
2	cups broccoli flowerets
1	cup thinly sliced yellow summer squash or zucchini
1	cup frozen peas
¾	cup chicken broth
⅓	cup dry white wine or chicken broth
2	tablespoons cornstarch
¼	teaspoon dried thyme, crushed
⅛	teaspoon pepper
1	medium tomato
2	tablespoons grated Parmesan cheese

- Thaw fish fillets, if frozen. Cut fish fillets into 1-inch pieces; set aside. Cook the pasta according to the directions on page 9. Drain the pasta; return to pan and cover to keep warm.

- Meanwhile, place broccoli and squash in a steamer basket set over boiling water. Cover and steam for 3 minutes. Carefully add peas to steamer basket. Cover and steam for 3 to 4 minutes more or until vegetables are crisp-tender. Remove steamer basket from pan.

- Combine chicken broth, wine or chicken broth, cornstarch, thyme, and pepper in a medium saucepan. Cook and stir until thickened and bubbly. Add fish. Cook for 3 to 5 minutes more or until fish just flakes when tested with a fork, stirring gently once or twice.

- Seed and chop tomato; set aside. Add the steamed vegetables to the pasta. Toss gently to mix.

- To serve, transfer pasta mixture to a warm serving dish. Pour the fish mixture over pasta mixture. Sprinkle with tomato and Parmesan cheese. Makes 4 servings.

Fish and
Shells Stew

Per serving:
266 cal. (7% from fat), 25 g pro., 38 g carbo., 2 g fat,
34 mg cholesterol, 8 g dietary fiber, 1,331 mg sodium.

Preparation time:
30 minutes

Switch to Cajun- or Italian-style stewed tomatoes, and this satisfying supper takes on a completely different—but every bit as delicious—flavor.

12	ounces fresh or frozen skinless fish fillets*
1	15-ounce can pinto beans
2	14½-ounce cans beef broth
1	cup frozen cut green beans
2	ounces packaged dried medium shells (about ⅔ cup)
½	cup chopped onion
1	teaspoon dried marjoram or basil, crushed
1	14½-ounce can Mexican-style stewed tomatoes

- Thaw fish fillets, if frozen. Cut fish fillets into 1-inch pieces; set aside.

- Rinse and drain pinto beans. Combine pinto beans, beef broth, green beans, *uncooked* pasta, onion, marjoram, and ¼ teaspoon *pepper* in a large saucepan. Bring to boiling; reduce heat. Cover and simmer for 10 minutes.

- Stir in *undrained* stewed tomatoes and fish. Return to boiling; reduce heat. Cover and simmer for 2 to 3 minutes or until fish just flakes when tested with a fork. Makes 4 servings.

*Use cod, pike, or orange roughy fillets.

Chicken Tortellini Soup

Chicken Tortellini Soup

Per serving:
250 cal. (25% from fat), 28 g pro., 19 g carbo., 7 g fat,
63 mg cholesterol, 3 g dietary fiber, 1,039 mg sodium.

**Preparation time:
20 minutes**

The flavor of this attractive soup depends on the blend of vegetables you use. Choose a prepackaged frozen mixture or combine two or three of your favorite frozen vegetables to measure 1½ cups.

2   14½-ounce cans chicken broth

½   of a 7-ounce package dried cheese tortellini (about 1 cup)*

¾   cup water

Several dashes bottled hot pepper sauce

1½   cups frozen loose-pack vegetables

2   cups cubed cooked chicken breast

● Combine chicken broth, *uncooked* pasta, water, and hot pepper sauce in a large saucepan. Bring to boiling; reduce heat. Cook, covered, for 5 minutes. Add frozen vegetables. Return to boiling; reduce heat. Cover and simmer for 5 minutes more.

● Add chicken and cook about 5 minutes more or until pasta and vegetables are tender. Makes 4 servings.

*To use refrigerated tortellini, substitute a 9-ounce package for the dried tortellini and skip the first 5 minutes of cooking.

Creamy Crab and Pasta

Per serving:
248 cal. (23% from fat), 22 g pro., 25 g carbo., 6 g fat,
100 mg cholesterol, 1 g dietary fiber, 482 mg sodium.

**Preparation time:
20 minutes**

**Baking time:
15 minutes**

Try making this recipe with 12 ounces of crab-flavored salad-style fish instead of canned crabmeat. Look for the crab-flavored fish in the deli or frozen-food section of your supermarket.

3   ounces packaged dried medium noodles

½   cup chopped celery

¼   cup chopped green pepper

2   tablespoons sliced green onions

1   cup skim milk

2   tablespoons all-purpose flour

1   teaspoon Worcestershire sauce

½   teaspoon dried thyme, crushed

Several dashes bottled hot pepper sauce

2   6½-ounce cans crabmeat, drained, flaked, and cartilage removed

2   tablespoons chopped pimiento

Crumb Topping (see recipe, above right)

● Cook the pasta according to the directions on page 9. Drain the pasta; cover to keep warm.

● Meanwhile, combine celery, green pepper, green onions, and ¼ cup *water* in a saucepan. Cover and cook until vegetables are just tender. Combine skim milk, flour, Worcestershire sauce, thyme, hot pepper sauce, and ⅛ teaspoon *salt* in a small bowl. Stir into vegetables. Cook and stir until thickened and bubbly. Stir in crabmeat and pimiento.

● Divide cooked pasta among four 8- to 10-ounce baking dishes. Spoon crab mixture over pasta. Sprinkle with Crumb Topping. Bake, uncovered, in a 350° oven about 15 minutes or until heated through. Makes 4 servings.

Crumb Topping: Stir together 2 tablespoons grated *Parmesan cheese*, 2 tablespoons *fine dry bread crumbs*, and 1 tablespoon melted *margarine* or *butter* in a bowl.

Sautéed Garlic Scallops with Dried Tomatoes

Per serving:
321 cal. (19% from fat), 24 g pro., 41 g carbo., 7 g fat,
43 mg cholesterol, 2 g dietary fiber, 445 mg sodium.

Preparation time:
35 minutes

Dried tomatoes add a delightfully refreshing flavor to this sophisticated main dish.

1	pound fresh or frozen bay or sea scallops
6	dried tomato halves (not oil-packed)
⅓	cup boiling water
6	ounces packaged dried fettuccine
2	teaspoons cooking oil
3	large cloves garlic, minced
2	cups sliced fresh mushrooms
4	green onions, sliced
2	tablespoons snipped parsley
½	teaspoon finely shredded lemon peel
2	tablespoons lemon juice
2	teaspoons cornstarch

- Thaw scallops, if frozen. Combine dried tomatoes and boiling water in a small bowl. Let stand 10 minutes. Drain tomatoes, reserving liquid. Cut tomatoes into thin strips. Set aside.

- Cook the pasta according to the directions on page 9. Drain the pasta; cover to keep warm.

- Meanwhile, pour oil into a large nonstick skillet; preheat over medium-high heat. Stir-fry garlic in hot oil for 15 seconds. Add mushrooms. Stir-fry for 2 minutes. Add scallops and tomatoes. Stir-fry for 2 to 3 minutes more or until scallops are opaque. Stir in reserved tomato liquid, the green onions, snipped parsley, and lemon peel.

- Combine lemon juice and cornstarch in a small bowl. Add to skillet. Cook and stir until slightly thickened and bubbly. Cook and stir for 1 minute more.

- Serve scallop mixture over pasta. Garnish with parsley sprigs, if desired. Makes 4 servings.

Chili-Sauced Pasta

Per serving:
320 cal. (5% from fat), 15 g pro., 64 g carbo., 2 g fat,
8 mg cholesterol, 12 g dietary fiber, 820 mg sodium.

Preparation time:
25 minutes

Chili fans at your house will request this linguine with a Tex-Mex twist often.

4	ounces packaged dried linguine
1	14½-ounce can stewed tomatoes
1	medium green pepper, cut into thin strips
2	tablespoons tomato paste
1	tablespoon chili powder
¼	teaspoon salt
¼	teaspoon garlic powder
¼	teaspoon ground cumin
1	8-ounce can red kidney beans
¼	cup cold water
2	teaspoons cornstarch

- Cook the pasta according to the directions on page 9. Drain the pasta; cover to keep warm.

- Meanwhile, combine *undrained* stewed tomatoes, green pepper, tomato paste, chili powder, salt, garlic powder, and cumin in a medium saucepan. Bring to boiling; reduce heat. Cover and simmer for 3 minutes. Rinse and drain kidney beans; stir into tomato mixture.

- Stir together cold water and cornstarch in a small bowl; add to tomato mixture. Cook and stir until thickened and bubbly. Cook and stir for 2 minutes more.

- Serve the tomato mixture over pasta. Makes 3 servings.

Vegetable-Macaroni Casserole

Per serving:
262 cal. (11% from fat), 16 g pro., 44 g carbo., 3 g fat,
8 mg cholesterol, 4 g dietary fiber, 471 mg sodium.

Preparation time:
25 minutes

Baking time:
15 minutes

Standing time:
5 minutes

Creamy, well-seasoned, and full of vegetables perfectly describes this healthy, home-style dish.

1   medium zucchini

3   ounces packaged dried elbow macaroni*

1   10-ounce package frozen mixed vegetables

1   12-ounce can evaporated skim milk

½   cup chicken broth

¼   cup all-purpose flour

½   teaspoon dried oregano, crushed

¼   teaspoon garlic salt

    Nonstick spray coating

1   medium tomato, sliced

¼   cup grated Parmesan cheese

- Halve the zucchini lengthwise; slice. Cook the pasta according to the directions on page 9, adding mixed vegetables and zucchini during the last 3 minutes of cooking time. Drain the pasta mixture; return to the pan.

- Meanwhile, stir together evaporated skim milk, chicken broth, flour, oregano, garlic salt, and ⅛ teaspoon *pepper* in a medium saucepan. Cook and stir until thickened and bubbly. Add to the pasta mixture; toss to coat.

- Spray a 2-quart square baking dish with nonstick spray coating. Pour the pasta mixture into the dish. Bake, uncovered, in a 375° oven for 10 minutes.

- Top with sliced tomato and sprinkle with Parmesan cheese. Bake, uncovered, about 5 minutes more or until heated through. Let stand for 5 minutes before serving. Makes 4 servings.

*Pasta should measure ¾ cup.

Cheese Spirals with Tomato Sauce

Per serving:
299 cal. (21% from fat), 16 g pro., 43 g carbo., 7 g fat,
20 mg cholesterol, 2 g dietary fiber, 579 mg sodium.

Preparation time:
40 minutes

Cooking time:
12 minutes

These eye-catching pasta rolls are brimming with a savory three-cheese filling.

8   packaged dried lasagna noodles

½   cup part-skim or nonfat ricotta cheese, drained

½   cup shredded part-skim mozzarella cheese

2   tablespoons grated Parmesan cheese

1½ teaspoons dried basil, crushed

½   teaspoon dried marjoram, crushed

1   egg white

1   14½-ounce can stewed tomatoes

¼   teaspoon salt

1   tablespoon cold water

1   teaspoon cornstarch

- Cook, rinse, and drain the pasta according to the directions on page 9.

- Meanwhile, for filling, combine ricotta cheese, mozzarella cheese, Parmesan cheese, *1 teaspoon* basil, and the marjoram in a medium mixing bowl. Slightly beat egg white; stir into ricotta mixture, mixing well. Spread about *2 tablespoons* of the filling on *each* lasagna noodle. Roll each noodle up from one end.

- Combine *undrained* stewed tomatoes, *½ teaspoon* basil, and salt in a large skillet. Bring to boiling. Combine water and cornstarch in a small bowl; add to tomato mixture. Cook and stir until thickened and bubbly.

- Place the lasagna rolls, seam side down, in the skillet. Cover and simmer for 12 to 15 minutes or until heated through. Makes 4 servings.

Broccoli Lasagna

Per serving:
344 cal. (27% from fat), 23 g pro., 39 g carbo., 10 g fat,
35 mg cholesterol, 2 g dietary fiber, 655 mg sodium.

Preparation time:
35 minutes

Baking time:
30 minutes

Standing time:
10 minutes

Cut down on fat but not on flavor with this zesty meatless lasagna.

9	packaged dried lasagna noodles
1	10-ounce package frozen chopped broccoli
1¾	cups skim milk
2	tablespoons cornstarch
1	tablespoon dried minced onion
2	teaspoons instant chicken bouillon granules
1	15-ounce container part-skim or nonfat ricotta cheese, drained
2	tablespoons grated Parmesan cheese
1	teaspoon dried basil, crushed
¼	teaspoon garlic powder
1	4½-ounce jar sliced mushrooms, drained
1	cup shredded part-skim mozzarella cheese

- Cook and drain the pasta according to the directions on page 9. Cook frozen broccoli according to the package directions; drain thoroughly.

- Meanwhile, for sauce, combine skim milk, cornstarch, dried onion, and bouillon granules in a medium saucepan. Cook and stir until thickened and bubbly.

- Combine ricotta cheese, Parmesan cheese, basil, and garlic powder in a medium mixing bowl.

- Spread ¼ *cup* of the sauce evenly on the bottom of a 2-quart rectangular baking dish. Place *3* noodles in the dish. (Trim noodles, if necessary.) Spread with *a third* of the remaining sauce. Layer with *half* of the broccoli, *half* of the ricotta cheese mixture, and *half* of the mushrooms. Sprinkle with a *fourth* of the mozzarella cheese. Add *3* more lasagna noodles. Spread with another *third* of the sauce. Layer with the remaining broccoli, ricotta mixture, and mushrooms. Sprinkle with another *fourth* of the mozzarella cheese. Add the remaining noodles. Top with the remaining sauce.

- Cover and bake in a 375° oven for 15 minutes. Sprinkle with the remaining mozzarella cheese. Bake, uncovered, for 15 to 20 minutes more or until heated through. Let stand for 10 minutes before serving. Makes 6 servings.

Spaghetti alla Carbonara

Per serving:
327 cal. (16% from fat), 17 g pro., 51 g carbo., 6 g fat,
77 mg cholesterol, 2 g dietary fiber, 310 mg sodium.

Preparation time:
30 minutes

If you like Italian cooking, you'll love this low-fat version of a pasta classic.

8	ounces packaged dried spaghetti or linguine
	Nonstick spray coating
2	slices turkey bacon
1	beaten egg
¾	cup evaporated skim milk
½	cup frozen peas
¼	cup chopped red sweet pepper
⅛	teaspoon crushed red pepper
¼	cup freshly shredded Parmesan cheese
	Cracked black pepper

- Cook pasta according to the directions on page 9. Drain the pasta; cover to keep warm.

- Meanwhile, spray a medium saucepan with nonstick coating. Halve turkey bacon slices. Cook in saucepan until crisp and light brown. Drain on paper towels. Wipe saucepan clean with paper towel. Crumble bacon.

- Combine egg, evaporated skim milk, peas, sweet pepper, and crushed red pepper in the same saucepan used to cook bacon. Cook and stir over medium heat just until mixture coats a metal spoon (about 6 minutes). *Do not boil.* Stir in *half* of the bacon and *half* of the Parmesan. Gently toss egg mixture and pasta until pasta is coated.

- To serve, transfer to a warm serving platter. Sprinkle with cracled black pepper, remaining bacon, and remaining Parmesan cheese. Makes 4 servings.

Note: Pictured on pages 58–59.

Broccoli Lasagna

Sensational
Side Dishes

Accompany meals with simple, speedy pasta dishes that add flavor and variety. This chapter offers salads, vegetable tosses, and appetizer soups for everyday meals or special occasions. And when time is really crunched, try one of the quick pasta fix-ups on page 93 for a tasty side dish in minutes.

Pesto Pasta Salad made with carrot fettuccine (See recipe, page 78.)

Pesto Pasta Salad

Per serving:
313 cal. (58% from fat), 9 g pro., 25 g carbo., 21 g fat,
7 mg cholesterol, 3 g dietary fiber, 218 mg sodium.

Preparation time:
20 minutes

The distinctive flavor of pesto highlights this easy salad. For a colorful combo, use carrot fettuccine.

2 ounces packaged dried fettuccine

½ of a 7-ounce container refrigerated pesto sauce

1 tablespoon lemon juice

½ cup coarsely chopped, seeded tomato

1 small red onion, thinly sliced

Torn fresh spinach

2 tablespoons pine nuts or slivered almonds, toasted

Basil sprigs (optional)

- Cook, rinse, and drain the pasta according to the directions on page 9.

- Combine pesto sauce and lemon juice in a large mixing bowl. Add the pasta; toss gently until pasta is coated.

- Add tomato and red onion to the pasta mixture; toss until mixed.

- To serve, line a serving platter with torn spinach. Spoon the pasta mixture onto the spinach. Sprinkle pasta mixture with toasted nuts. Garnish with basil sprigs, if desired. Makes 3 servings.

Note: Pictured on pages 76–77 made with carrot fettuccine.

Curried Broccoli and Pasta

Per serving:
165 cal. (25% from fat), 7 g pro., 25 g carbo., 5 g fat,
2 mg cholesterol, 2 g dietary fiber, 169 mg sodium.

Preparation time:
25 minutes

Complement the zippy taste of this side dish with baked or broiled chicken breasts or fish, a fruit salad, and French bread.

3 ounces packaged dried corkscrew macaroni (about 1⅓ cups)

1 tablespoon olive or cooking oil

1 teaspoon curry powder

3 cups broccoli flowerets

½ cup chopped red or green sweet pepper

½ cup plain yogurt

⅓ cup chicken broth

4 teaspoons all-purpose flour

1 teaspoon prepared mustard

Dash salt

- Cook, rinse, and drain the pasta according to the directions on page 9.

- Meanwhile, heat oil in a large skillet over medium-high heat. Add curry powder and stir-fry for 1 minute. Add broccoli and sweet pepper; stir-fry for 3 to 4 minutes or until the vegetables are crisp-tender. Remove from heat.

- Stir together yogurt, chicken broth, flour, mustard, and salt in a small mixing bowl. Stir into the broccoli mixture. Cook and stir until thickened and bubbly. Cook and stir for 1 minute more. Add the pasta to broccoli mixture; toss to mix. Heat through. Makes 4 servings.

Zesty Vegetable-
Pasta Toss

Per serving:
157 cal. (18% from fat), 7 g pro., 24 g carbo., 3 g fat,
7 mg cholesterol, 3 g dietary fiber, 276 mg sodium.

**Preparation time:
25 minutes**

Fresh herbs, a fiery chili
pepper, and sharp asiago
cheese combine to give
this vegetable-packed side
dish great gusto.

4   ounces packaged dried
    fusilli, broken in half

⅓   cup dry white wine or
    chicken broth

¼   teaspoon salt

    Nonstick spray coating

1½ cups carrots cut into
    2-inch-long strips

1½ cups fresh green beans
    diagonally cut into
    2-inch lengths

½   cup leeks cut into
    ½-inch slices

1   tablespoon fresh
    snipped basil or
    1 teaspoon dried basil,
    crushed

1   tablespoon fresh
    snipped dill or
    1 teaspoon dried
    dillweed

1   clove garlic, minced

1½ cups yellow summer
    squash cut into 2-inch-
    long strips

2   tablespoons water

1   fresh red cayenne chili
    pepper, seeded and
    finely chopped
    (½ teaspoon)*

½   cup finely shredded
    asiago or Parmesan
    cheese

● Cook the pasta according to the directions on page 9.
Drain the pasta; cover to keep warm.

● Meanwhile, combine wine or chicken broth and salt; set
aside. Spray a wok or large skillet with nonstick spray
coating. Preheat over medium heat. Add carrot strips,
green beans, leek slices, basil, dill, and garlic. Stir-fry
for 3 minutes.

● Add yellow squash, water, and finely chopped fresh red
pepper to the wok. Cover and cook for 5 to 6 minutes
more or until the vegetables are crisp-tender.

● Add the pasta to vegetables. Drizzle with wine mixture.
Toss gently.

● To serve, transfer to a warm serving platter. Sprinkle
with finely shredded asiago or Parmesan cheese.
Garnish with additional fresh red cayenne chili peppers,
if desired. Makes 6 servings.

*If desired, substitute ⅛ teaspoon ground red pepper for
the fresh cayenne chili pepper. When using the ground
red pepper, add it with the wine.

Handle Peppers with Care

Use caution when working with hot chili peppers, such as red
cayenne chili peppers, jalapeños, and serranos—the oils from
the peppers can burn your skin and eyes. Always wear plastic or
rubber gloves when seeding or chopping the peppers (or slip a
plastic bag over each hand) and don't touch or rub your eyes.
Also, remember to wash your hands and nails thoroughly with
soap and water after you've finished working with the peppers.

Ziti with Blue Cheese Sauce

Ziti with Blue Cheese Sauce

Per serving:
195 cal. (46% from fat), 7 g pro., 19 g carbo., 10 g fat,
16 mg cholesterol, 0 g dietary fiber, 258 mg sodium.

Preparation time:
20 minutes

This tangy pasta dish tastes great alongside broiled steak or pork chops.

3 ounces packaged dried cut ziti* or corkscrew macaroni (about 1 cup)

3 cups loose-pack frozen broccoli, cauliflower, and carrots

2 tablespoons margarine or butter

2 tablespoons all-purpose flour

1/8 teaspoon salt

1/8 teaspoon pepper

1 cup milk

1/2 cup crumbled blue cheese (2 ounces)

1/3 cup dairy sour cream

- Cook the pasta according to the directions on page 9, adding the frozen vegetables during the last 5 to 7 minutes of the cooking time. Drain the pasta mixture; cover to keep warm.

- Meanwhile, melt margarine or butter in a small saucepan. Stir in flour, salt, and pepper. Add milk all at once. Cook and stir until thickened and bubbly. Cook and stir for 1 minute more. Remove from heat. Stir in blue cheese and the sour cream.

- To serve, gently toss the blue cheese mixture with pasta-vegetable mixture until pasta is coated. Garnish with a cilantro or parsley sprig, if desired. Makes 6 servings.

*If you can't find cut ziti, buy the long kind and break into 1-inch lengths before cooking.

Mostaccioli with Tomatoes

Per serving:
186 cal. (11% from fat), 7 g pro., 35 g carbo., 2 g fat,
2 mg cholesterol, 2 g dietary fiber, 257 mg sodium.

Preparation time:
35 minutes

The flavors of fresh rosemary, garlic, and red hot pepper saturate this tantalizing tomato sauce.

2 tablespoons fresh snipped rosemary or 1 teaspoon dried rosemary, crushed

2 to 4 cloves garlic, minced

1 tablespoon cooking oil

1 28-ounce can tomatoes, cut up

1 small dried red hot pepper or 1/8 teaspoon ground red pepper

1/2 teaspoon sugar

8 ounces packaged dried mostaccioli

2 tablespoons grated Parmesan cheese

- Cook rosemary and garlic in hot oil in a large skillet until the garlic is golden. Stir in *undrained* tomatoes, whole or ground red pepper, and sugar. Bring to boiling; reduce heat. Simmer, uncovered, about 20 minutes or until desired consistency, stirring occasionally.

- Meanwhile, cook the pasta according to the directions on page 9. Drain the pasta; cover to keep warm.

- If used, remove the whole red pepper from the sauce and discard. Gently toss the tomato mixture with pasta until pasta is coated. Serve with Parmesan. Makes 6 servings.

Creamy Pesto Pasta

Per serving:
203 cal. (40% from fat), 7 g pro., 23 g carbo., 9 g fat,
19 mg cholesterol, 0 g dietary fiber, 138 mg sodium.

Preparation time:
25 minutes

This light, fresh-tasting sauce is especially appealing on warm days.

6 ounces packaged dried rigatoni or mostaccioli

2 tablespoons fresh snipped basil or 2 teaspoons dried basil, crushed

1 clove garlic, minced

1 tablespoon olive or cooking oil

1 3-ounce package cream cheese

¼ cup drained cottage cheese

3 tablespoons grated Parmesan cheese

2 tablespoons snipped parsley

2 tablespoons dry white wine or chicken broth

- Cook the pasta according to the directions on page 9. Drain the pasta; cover to keep warm.

- Meanwhile, cook basil and garlic in hot oil in a medium saucepan for 1 minute. Reduce heat. Add cream cheese, cottage cheese, and Parmesan cheese. Heat and stir until fairly smooth.

- Stir parsley, wine or chicken broth, and 3 tablespoons *water* into saucepan. Cook, uncovered, over medium heat about 3 minutes or until slightly thickened.

- Serve the basil mixture over pasta. Garnish with basil sprigs, if desired. Makes 6 servings.

Herbed Pasta with Vegetables

Per serving:
171 cal. (46% from fat), 4 g pro., 19 g carbo., 9 g fat,
0 mg cholesterol, 0 g dietary fiber, 147 mg sodium.

Preparation time:
20 minutes

This orange-flavored sauce is so versatile it complements any frozen vegetable combination that strikes your fancy.

3 ounces packaged dried medium shells (about 1 cup)

1½ cups loose-pack frozen broccoli, French-style green beans, onions, and red sweet pepper*

3 tablespoons margarine or butter

1 tablespoon snipped parsley

1 clove garlic, minced

1 teaspoon finely shredded orange peel

½ teaspoon dried thyme, crushed

⅛ teaspoon salt

Dash ground red pepper

- Cook the pasta according to the directions on page 9, adding the frozen vegetables during the last 5 minutes of cooking time. Drain pasta mixture; cover to keep warm.

- Meanwhile, melt the margarine or butter in a small saucepan. Stir in parsley, garlic, orange peel, thyme, salt, and ground red pepper.

- To serve, gently toss thyme mixture with pasta-vegetable mixture until pasta is coated. Makes 4 servings.

*If you like, substitute 1½ cups of any frozen vegetable combination.

Fettuccine with Basil-Parmesan Sauce

Per serving:
230 cal. (28% from fat), 9 g pro., 32 g carbo., 7 g fat,
22 mg cholesterol, 1 g dietary fiber, 138 mg sodium.

**Preparation time:
25 minutes**

Easy and elegant at the same time, this sumptuous dish takes only one pan to cook.

8   ounces packaged dried fettuccine or linguine

1   tablespoon olive oil

¾   cup evaporated milk

⅓   cup grated Parmesan cheese

¼   cup sliced green onions

2   tablespoons fresh snipped basil or 2 teaspoons dried basil, crushed

¼   teaspoon finely shredded lemon peel

¼   teaspoon garlic powder

⅛   teaspoon pepper

- Cook the pasta according to the directions on page 9. Drain the pasta; return to the hot pan.

- Add olive oil to the pasta; toss to coat. Add evaporated milk, Parmesan cheese, green onions, basil, lemon peel, garlic powder, and pepper.

- Cook over medium-high heat until bubbly, stirring constantly. Season to taste with *salt*.

- To serve, transfer to a warm serving dish. Top with additional grated Parmesan cheese and a basil sprig, if desired. Makes 6 servings.

Pasta Smothered with Onions

Per serving:
211 cal. (37% from fat), 6 g pro., 24 g carbo., 9 g fat,
14 mg cholesterol, 1 g dietary fiber, 155 mg sodium.

**Preparation time:
40 minutes**

For this special dish, try a sweet variety of onion, such as Vidalia, Walla Walla, or Texas Spring Sweet. Creamy Bel Paese rounds out the sweet mellow flavor of the onions.

2   medium onions, cut into thin wedges

1   clove garlic, minced

2   tablespoons margarine or butter

⅓   cup chicken broth

¼   cup dry white wine or chicken broth

⅛   teaspoon pepper

4   ounces packaged dried linguine or fettuccine

¼   cup shredded Bel Paese or Gruyère cheese (1 ounce)

2   tablespoons snipped parsley

- Cook onions and garlic in margarine or butter in a covered, medium saucepan over low heat about 20 minutes or until onions are very tender, stirring occasionally. Uncover and cook over medium-high heat about 10 minutes more or until the onions are a deep golden color, stirring frequently.

- Stir chicken broth, wine, and pepper into saucepan. Boil gently, uncovered, for 6 to 8 minutes or until most of the liquid is evaporated; stir frequently.

- Meanwhile, cook the pasta according to the directions on page 9. Drain the pasta; return to the hot pan.

- Add the onion mixture to the pasta in the pan. Add Bel Paese or Gruyère cheese and parsley. Place the pan over low heat. Gently toss until the pasta is well coated and the mixture is heated through. Makes 4 servings.

Summer Vegetables with Linguine

Per serving:
189 cal. (30% from fat), 6 g pro., 25 g carbo., 6 g fat,
9 mg cholesterol, 2 g dietary fiber, 171 mg sodium.

**Preparation time:
25 minutes**

Wow your guests by making this luscious dish with a colorful combination of regular and spinach linguine. For an entrée, grill halibut or salmon steaks or chicken breasts.

1   medium yellow summer squash

1   medium zucchini

1   medium red sweet pepper

6   ounces packaged dried linguine

¼   cup dry white wine or chicken broth

¼   teaspoon salt

¼   teaspoon dried basil, crushed

¼   teaspoon dried tarragon, crushed

¼   teaspoon crushed red pepper

2   tablespoons olive oil

1½ cups sliced fresh mushrooms

2   or 3 cloves garlic, minced

¼   cup freshly grated Parmesan cheese

● Cut yellow squash and zucchini into thirds lengthwise; cut each third into ¼-inch-thick slices. Cut red sweet pepper into thin strips. Set aside.

● Cook the pasta according to the directions on page 9. Drain the pasta; cover to keep warm.

● Combine the white wine or chicken broth, salt, basil, tarragon, and crushed red pepper; set aside

● Meanwhile, pour olive oil into a wok or large skillet; preheat over medium-high heat. Add yellow squash, zucchini, red sweet pepper, mushrooms, and garlic. Stir-fry for 2 to 3 minutes or until the vegetables are crisp-tender.

● Stir wine mixture. Drizzle the mixture over vegetables; toss to coat. Heat through.

● To serve, gently toss the pasta with vegetable mixture until well mixed. Transfer to a large warm serving platter. Sprinkle with freshly grated Parmesan cheese. Makes 6 to 8 servings.

Note: Also pictured on the cover.

Let Your Microwave Help

On hot summer days—or just for a change of pace—cook the vegetable combination for the recipe above in the microwave oven instead of in a wok or skillet.

Combine yellow squash slices, zucchini slices, red sweet pepper strips, mushrooms, and garlic (omit the olive oil) in the Tupperware® 1¾-quart TupperWave® casserole. Micro-cook, covered, on 100% power (high) for 5 to 7 minutes or until vegetables are crisp-tender, stirring once. Drain excess liquid.

Stir together wine, salt, basil, tarragon, and crushed red pepper. Drizzle the mixture over vegetables; toss to coat. Cook, covered, on high for 30 to 60 seconds more or until heated through. Continue as directed above.

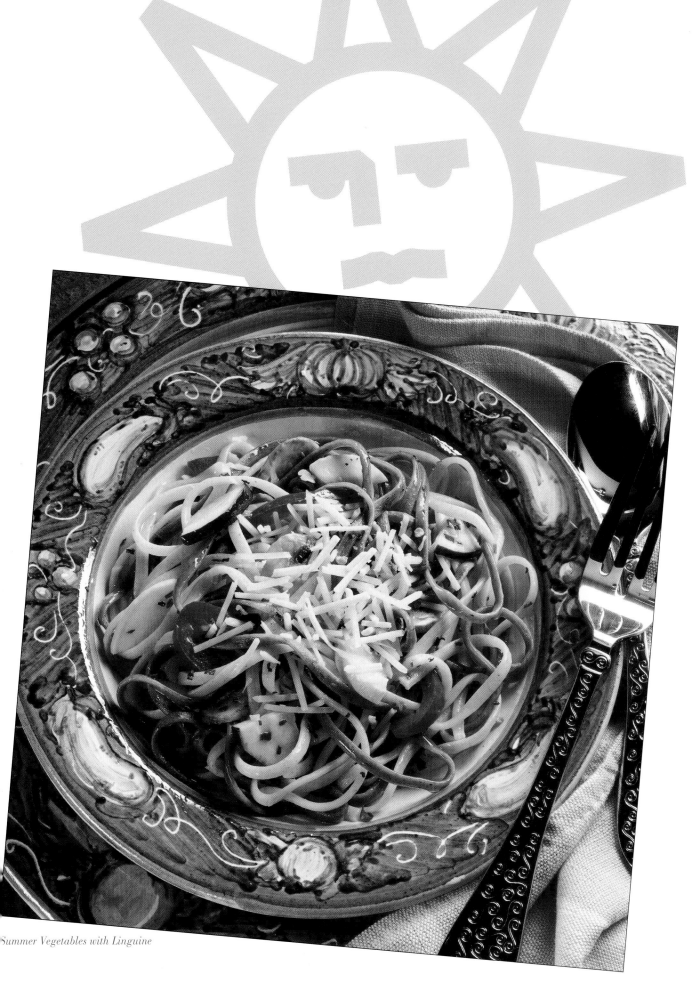

Summer Vegetables with Linguine

Pasta with Whisky-Cream Sauce

Per serving:
442 cal. (46% from fat), 7 g pro., 36 g carbo., 23 g fat,
61 mg cholesterol, 1 g dietary fiber, 210 mg sodium.

Preparation time:
25 minutes

For a celebration dinner, serve this sophisticated dish with beef or chicken kabobs.

1   medium onion, thinly sliced

1   stalk celery, chopped

¼   cup snipped chives

1   clove garlic, minced

2   tablespoons margarine or butter

½   cup Scotch whisky or bourbon

¼   teaspoon salt

⅛   teaspoon pepper

¾   cup whipping cream

6   ounces packaged dried spaghetti or spaghettini

Grated Parmesan cheese (optional)

- Cook the onion, celery, chives, and garlic in the margarine or butter in a medium saucepan until the vegetables are tender.

- Add Scotch whisky or bourbon, salt, and pepper to the vegetable mixture. Bring to boiling; reduce heat. Simmer, uncovered, about 12 minutes or until most of the liquid is evaporated, stirring occasionally. Stir in whipping cream. Cook and stir about 5 minutes more or until sauce thickens.

- Meanwhile, cook the pasta according to the directions on page 9. Drain the pasta.

- To serve, gently toss the pasta with whisky mixture until pasta is coated. Sprinkle with Parmesan cheese, if desired. Makes 4 servings.

Herbed Cauliflower and Pasta

Per serving:
215 cal. (20% from fat), 8 g pro., 37 g carbo., 5 g fat,
0 mg cholesterol, 2 g dietary fiber, 76 mg sodium.

Preparation time:
25 minutes

Pine nuts add unique flavor and texture to this simple side dish. Serve it with broiled lamb chops.

1½   ounces packaged dried corkscrew macaroni (about ½ cup)

3   cups small cauliflower or broccoli flowerets

1   teaspoon fresh snipped rosemary or ¼ teaspoon dried rosemary, crushed

2   tablespoons pine nuts

2   teaspoons olive or cooking oil

⅛   teaspoon garlic salt

⅛   teaspoon pepper

- Cook the pasta according to the directions on page 9, adding the cauliflower or broccoli and rosemary during the last 5 minutes of cooking time. Drain the pasta mixture; return to the hot pan.

- Add pine nuts, oil, garlic salt, and pepper to the pasta mixture. Toss to mix. Makes 4 servings.

Italian-Style Zucchini and Pasta

Per serving:
154 cal. (40% from fat), 3 g pro., 21 g carbo., 7 g fat,
0 mg cholesterol, 1 g dietary fiber, 366 mg sodium.

**Preparation time:
25 minutes**

Fennel seed and crushed red pepper stamp the flavor of Italy on this zucchini and pasta dish.

1½   ounces packaged dried cavatelli (about ½ cup)

1   cup chopped onion

¼   cup thinly sliced or coarsely chopped carrot

1   clove garlic, minced

2   tablespoons olive or cooking oil

1   14½-ounce can Italian-style stewed tomatoes

1   small zucchini, halved lengthwise and cut into ¼-inch-thick slices

½   teaspoon fennel seed, crushed

⅛   to ¼ teaspoon crushed red pepper

- Cook, rinse, and drain the pasta according to the directions on page 9.

- Meanwhile, cook onion, carrot, and garlic in hot oil in a large skillet about 5 minutes or until the vegetables are crisp-tender.

- Stir *undrained* stewed tomatoes, zucchini, fennel seed, and crushed red pepper into the skillet. Bring to boiling; reduce heat. Simmer, uncovered, for 3 minutes. Stir in the pasta; heat through. Makes 4 servings.

Fusilli and Vegetable Toss

Per serving:
186 cal. (28% from fat), 6 g pro., 29 g carbo., 6 g fat,
0 mg cholesterol, 1 g dietary fiber, 42 mg sodium.

**Preparation time:
25 minutes**

Turn this delicious side dish into a hearty main dish for two by adding 1½ cups of chopped cooked chicken.

4   ounces packaged dried fusilli or spaghetti

2   cups sliced fresh mushrooms

⅓   cup finely chopped onion

1   clove garlic, minced

1   tablespoon olive or cooking oil

1   medium zucchini, halved lengthwise and cut into ¼-inch-thick slices

½   cup oil-packed dried tomatoes, drained and chopped

½   teaspoon dried Italian seasoning, crushed

     Shredded Parmesan cheese (optional)

- Cook the pasta according to the directions on page 9. Drain the pasta; cover to keep warm.

- Meanwhile, cook mushrooms, onion, and garlic in hot oil in a large skillet until the vegetables are tender.

- Add zucchini, dried tomatoes, and Italian seasoning to the skillet. Cook and stir for 2 to 3 minutes or until the zucchini is crisp-tender.

- Gently toss the vegetable mixture with pasta until well mixed. Transfer to a warm serving dish. Sprinkle with Parmesan cheese, if desired. Makes 4 servings.

Asparagus-Pasta Toss

Asparagus-Pasta Toss

Per serving:
129 cal. (35% from fat), 4 g pro., 18 g carbo., 5 g fat,
0 mg cholesterol, 1 g dietary fiber, 81 mg sodium.

Preparation time: 20 minutes

This easy side dish makes a super standby—just substitute whatever vegetable you have on hand for the asparagus.

4	ounces packaged dried medium bow ties
2	cups fresh asparagus cut into 1-inch pieces
¼	cup bottled Italian salad dressing
⅛	teaspoon pepper
½	cup chopped tomato
	Tarragon sprigs (optional)

- Cook the pasta according to the directions on page 9, adding asparagus during the last 5 minutes of cooking time. Drain the pasta mixture; return to the hot pan.

- Add Italian salad dressing and pepper to the pan, tossing to coat. Fold in the tomato.

- To serve, transfer to individual plates. Garnish with tarragon sprigs, if desired. Makes 6 servings.

Cashew Pasta Primavera

Per serving:
212 cal. (41% from fat), 7 g pro., 24 g carbo., 10 g fat,
7 mg cholesterol, 3 g dietary fiber, 170 mg sodium.

Preparation time: 25 minutes

Swirl vegetables, linguine, and cashews together for a mouthwatering side dish.

6	ounces packaged dried linguine or fettuccine
3	tablespoons margarine or butter
2	cups broccoli flowerets
1	cup bias-sliced carrots
1	medium onion, cut into thin wedges
1	clove garlic, minced
1	cup frozen pea pods
½	cup cashews or almonds
¼	cup dry white wine or chicken broth
1	teaspoon dried thyme, crushed
¼	teaspoon pepper
¼	cup grated Parmesan cheese

- Cook, rinse, and drain the pasta according to the directions on page 9.

- Meanwhile, melt *2 tablespoons* of the margarine or butter in a large skillet. Stir in broccoli, carrots, onion, and garlic. Cook and stir over medium-high heat about 3 minutes or until the broccoli is crisp-tender.

- Stir pea pods into skillet. Cook and stir for 2 minutes. Stir in the cooked pasta, remaining margarine or butter, the cashews or almonds, white wine or chicken broth, thyme, and pepper. Cover and cook for 1 minute more.

- To serve, transfer to a warm serving plate. Sprinkle with grated Parmesan cheese. Makes 8 servings.

Linguine with Marsala Tomato Sauce

Per serving:
238 cal. (34% from fat), 6 g pro., 31 g carbo., 9 g fat,
16 mg cholesterol, 3 g dietary fiber, 734 mg sodium.

**Preparation time:
25 minutes**

A touch of marsala wine
and bacon drippings give
this sauce a robust flavor.

2	slices bacon, cut into ½-inch pieces
1	small green pepper, chopped
1	clove garlic, minced
1	15-ounce can tomato sauce
¼	cup water
¼	cup dry marsala wine or beef broth
1	teaspoon sugar
½	teaspoon dried oregano, crushed
4	ounces packaged dried linguine

- Cook bacon pieces in a medium saucepan until crisp. Drain on paper towels, reserving drippings in saucepan. Set bacon aside.

- Cook green pepper and garlic in the reserved bacon drippings over medium heat until green pepper is tender but not brown. Stir in tomato sauce, water, marsala wine or beef broth, sugar, and oregano. Bring to boiling; reduce heat. Simmer, uncovered, for 15 to 20 minutes or until desired consistency, stirring occasionally.

- Meanwhile, cook the pasta according to the directions on page 9. Drain the pasta.

- Serve the tomato mixture over pasta. Sprinkle with bacon. Makes 4 servings.

Pasta and Vegetables with Vinaigrette

Per serving:
120 cal. (12% from fat), 4 g pro., 23 g carbo., 2 g fat,
0 mg cholesterol, 1 g dietary fiber, 142 mg sodium.

**Preparation time:
25 minutes**

Nicely tart, this dill-
flavored pasta dish is great
with grilled burgers
or chops.

3½	ounces packaged dried corkscrew macaroni (about 1⅓ cups)
1	cup sliced zucchini or yellow summer squash
1	small green pepper, cut into bite-size strips
1	clove garlic, minced
1	teaspoon olive or cooking oil
2	tablespoons white wine vinegar
½	teaspoon dried dillweed
¼	teaspoon salt
⅛	teaspoon ground black pepper
8	cherry tomatoes, halved

- Cook, rinse, and drain the pasta according to the directions on page 9.

- Meanwhile, halve any large slices of squash. Cook squash, green pepper, and garlic in hot oil in a large skillet about 3 minutes or until vegetables are tender.

- Add the pasta, vinegar, dillweed, salt, and black pepper to the skillet; toss to mix well. Add tomatoes. Cook and stir just until heated through. Makes 4 servings.

Angel Hair Pasta with Mushroom Sauce

Per serving:
230 cal. (44% from fat), 7 g pro., 26 g carbo., 11 g fat,
31 mg cholesterol, 1 g dietary fiber, 233 mg sodium.

**Preparation time:
15 minutes**

Angel hair pasta combines with a cream cheese-and-mushroom sauce for a side dish that's rich yet delicate.

4 ounces packaged dried angel hair pasta

1½ cups sliced fresh mushrooms

½ cup chopped onion

1 tablespoon margarine or butter

1 3-ounce package cream cheese, cut into cubes

¼ teaspoon salt

⅛ teaspoon pepper

⅓ cup milk

2 tablespoons snipped chives

- Cook the pasta according to the directions on page 9. Drain the pasta; return to the hot pan.

- Meanwhile, cook mushrooms and onion in margarine or butter in medium saucepan until vegetables are tender.

- Stir cream cheese, salt, and pepper into saucepan. Cook and stir over low heat until the cream cheese is melted. Gradually stir in milk and chives; heat through.

- To serve, gently toss the cheese mixture with pasta until pasta is coated. Makes 4 servings.

Gorgonzola-Sauced Vermicelli

Per serving:
257 cal. (47% from fat), 11 g pro., 23 g carbo., 14 g fat,
23 mg cholesterol, 0 g dietary fiber, 405 mg sodium.

**Preparation time:
20 minutes**

Gorgonzola cheese is soft and creamy with a less pungent flavor than blue cheese.

4 ounces packaged dried vermicelli

1 tablespoon margarine or butter

½ cup crumbled Gorgonzola or blue cheese (2 ounces)

¼ cup half-and-half, light cream, or milk

1 tablespoon fresh snipped basil or 1 teaspoon dried basil, crushed

   Dash white pepper

¼ cup grated Parmesan cheese

2 tablespoons toasted pine nuts or toasted chopped pecans

- Cook the pasta according to the directions on page 9. Drain the pasta; return to the hot pan.

- Meanwhile, melt margarine or butter in a small saucepan. Add Gorgonzola or blue cheese, half-and-half or light cream, basil, and white pepper. Cook and stir over medium heat just until the mixture is smooth and heated through. Stir in Parmesan cheese.

- To serve, gently toss the cheese mixture with pasta until pasta is coated. Transfer to a warm serving dish. Sprinkle with nuts. Makes 4 servings.

Asparagus-Pasta Bake

Per serving:
172 cal. (40% from fat), 7 g pro., 20 g carbo., 8 g fat,
14 mg cholesterol, 2 g dietary fiber, 446 mg sodium.

**Preparation time:
25 minutes**

**Baking time:
30 minutes**

When you know time is
going to be tight, assemble
and chill this creamy side-
dish casserole up to
24 hours ahead. Then bake
it for 35 to 40 minutes or
until hot.

4	ounces packaged dried spaghetti, broken
2	10-ounce packages frozen cut asparagus
1	10¾-ounce can condensed cream of celery soup
½	cup dairy sour cream
¼	cup milk
1	to 2 tablespoons Dijon-style mustard
1	2-ounce jar diced pimiento, drained
¼	cup grated Parmesan cheese
2	tablespoons fine dry bread crumbs
1	tablespoon margarine or butter, melted

- Cook, rinse, and drain the pasta according to the directions on page 9, adding the frozen asparagus during the last 2 minutes of cooking time.

- Stir together cream of celery soup, sour cream, milk, and Dijon-style mustard in a large mixing bowl. Stir in the pasta mixture, pimiento, and 3 *tablespoons* of the Parmesan cheese. Pour into a 2-quart rectangular baking dish.

- Stir together bread crumbs, melted margarine or butter, and the remaining Parmesan cheese in a small mixing bowl. Sprinkle over the pasta mixture.

- Bake, uncovered, in a 350° oven for 30 to 35 minutes or until heated through. Makes 8 servings.

Fresh Tomato Soup with Tortellini

Per serving:
154 cal. (43% from fat), 6 g pro., 18 g carbo., 8 g fat,
5 mg cholesterol, 3 g dietary fiber, 960 mg sodium.

**Preparation time:
30 minutes**

**Cooking time:
30 minutes**

Show off the best of
summer's fresh tomato
flavor in this appetizer or
side-dish soup.

6	ripe medium tomatoes
1	cup chopped onion
2	tablespoons margarine or butter
3	cups chicken broth
1	8-ounce can tomato sauce
1	teaspoon dried sage, crushed
¼	teaspoon salt
	Dash pepper
½	of a 7-ounce package dried cheese tortellini (about 1 cup)
¼	cup grated Parmesan cheese

- Peel, seed, and chop tomatoes. Cook onion in margarine or butter in a large saucepan until tender. Add tomatoes, chicken broth, tomato sauce, sage, salt, and pepper. Bring to boiling; reduce heat. Cover and simmer for 30 minutes. Cool slightly.

- Meanwhile, cook, rinse, and drain the pasta according to the directions on page 9.

- Press the tomato mixture through a food mill. (Or, place about *half* of the mixture in a blender container or food processor bowl. Cover and blend or process until smooth. Repeat with remaining mixture.)

- Return the tomato mixture to saucepan. Stir in the pasta; heat through.

- To serve, spoon the soup into individual bowls; sprinkle with grated Parmesan cheese. Makes 6 servings.

Fast Pasta Fix-Ups

Need a quick side dish? Just cook and drain 4 ounces of your favorite pasta (see directions on page 9), combine it with the ingredients from one of these ideas, and you're set—pasta for four in minutes!

Garlic-and-Caper Pasta: In the same hot pan used for the pasta, cook ½ teaspoon *bottled minced garlic* in 1 tablespoon hot *olive oil* for 15 seconds. Add ¼ cup chopped, drained *oil-packed dried tomatoes* and 1 tablespoon drained *capers.* Toss the garlic mixture and hot cooked pasta until mixed.
Per serving: 152 cal. (28% from fat), 4 g pro., 24 g carbo., 5 g fat, 0 mg cholesterol, 0 g dietary fiber, 56 mg sodium.

Pasta with Olives: In the same hot pan used for the pasta, toss 2 tablespoons grated *Parmesan* or *Romano cheese,* 1 tablespoon *margarine* or *butter,* and hot cooked pasta until well mixed. Stir in a few sliced pitted ripe or pimiento-stuffed *olives.*
Per serving: 149 cal. (28% from fat), 5 g pro., 22 g carbo., 5 g fat, 2 mg cholesterol, 0 g dietary fiber, 106 mg sodium.

Creamy Parmesan Pasta: In the same hot pan used for the pasta, combine 2 cups hot cooked *vegetables,* ⅓ cup grated *Parmesan cheese,* ⅓ cup *half-and-half* or *light cream,* and 2 tablespoons *margarine* or *butter.* Gently toss the vegetable mixture and hot cooked pasta until pasta is coated.
Per serving: 273 cal. (36% from fat), 10 g pro., 35 g carbo., 11 g fat, 14 mg cholesterol, 4 g dietary fiber, 243 mg sodium.

Pasta with Salami and Cheese: In the same hot pan used for the pasta, toss ½ cup shredded *mozzarella* or *provolone cheese,* ⅓ cup chopped *salami* or fully cooked *ham,* ⅓ cup *whipping cream,* and hot cooked pasta. Cook and stir over medium heat for 3 to 4 minutes or until cheese melts and sauce thickens slightly.
Per serving: 264 cal. (49% from fat), 11 g pro., 23 g carbo., 14 g fat, 44 mg cholesterol, 0 g dietary fiber, 314 mg sodium.

Parslied Pasta: In the same hot pan used for the pasta, cook ⅓ cup chopped *onion* and 1 tablespoon *dried parsley flakes* in 1 tablespoon *margarine* or *butter* until the onion is tender. Stir in ¼ teaspoon *garlic powder.* Toss onion mixture and hot cooked pasta until well mixed.
Per serving: 137 cal. (22% from fat), 4 g pro., 23 g carbo., 3 g fat, 0 mg cholesterol, 0 g dietary fiber, 28 mg sodium.

Poppy Seed and Orange Pasta: Combine ¼ teaspoon *finely shredded orange peel,* 3 tablespoons *orange juice,* 2 tablespoons *margarine* or *butter,* and 1½ teaspoons *poppy seed* in a small bowl. In same hot pan used for pasta, toss margarine mixture and hot cooked pasta until well mixed.
Per serving: 167 cal. (36% from fat), 4 g pro., 23 g carbo., 7 g fat, 0 mg cholesterol, 0 g dietary fiber, 50 mg sodium.

Two-Cheese Pasta: In the same hot pan used for the pasta, heat *half* of an 8-ounce container *soft-style cream cheese with chives and onion,* ¼ cup *milk,* and 1 tablespoon *dried parsley flakes* over medium-low heat until cream cheese melts and mixture is warm, stirring occasionally. Stir in ¼ cup grated *Parmesan* or *Romano cheese.* Toss the cheese mixture and hot cooked pasta until pasta is coated.
Per serving: 192 cal. (33% from fat), 8 g pro., 24 g carbo., 7 g fat, 6 mg cholesterol, 0 g dietary fiber, 207 mg sodium.

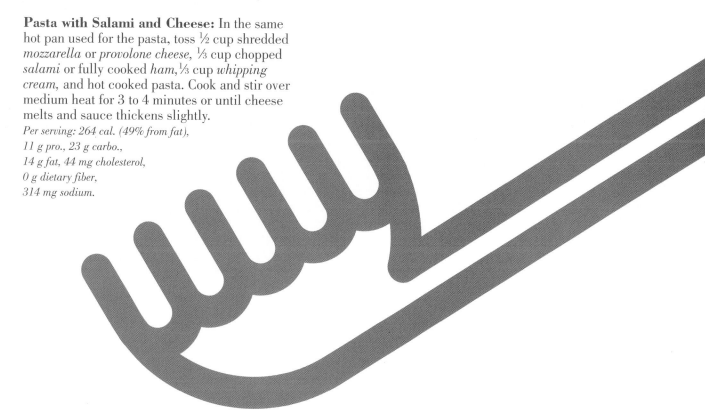

Index

Index (continued)

NUTRITIONAL FACTS

So you can keep track of what you eat, each recipe in this book lists the nutritional values for one serving. Here's how we made our analyses.

When a recipe gives a choice of ingredients (such as margarine or butter), we used the first choice in our analysis.

Ingredients listed as optional were omitted from our calculations.

Finally, we rounded all values to the nearest whole number.